Routledge Revivals

Studies in Economic Dynamics

First published in 1943, this work contains five interconnected essays presenting M. Kalecki's renowned additions to the business cycle theory.

Written by one of the most distinguished economists of the 20th century, this work will be essential reading for students and scholars of the history of economic thought, monetary theory and macroeconomics.

T0358557

Studies in Economic Dynamics

M. Kalecki

Routledge
Taylor & Francis Group

First published in 1943
by George Allen & Unwin Ltd

This edition first published in 2017 by Routledge
2 Park Square, Milton Park, Abingdon, Oxon, OX14 4RN
and by Routledge
711 Third Avenue, New York, NY 10017

Routledge is an imprint of the Taylor & Francis Group, an informa business

Publisher's Note
The publisher has gone to great lengths to ensure the quality of this
reprint but points out that some imperfections in the original copies may
be apparent.

Disclaimer
The publisher has made every effort to trace copyright holders and
welcomes correspondence from those they have been unable to contact.

A Library of Congress record exists under LC control number: 44001162

ISBN 13: 978-1-138-06447-8 (hbk)
ISBN 13: 978-1-315-16028-3 (ebk)

Studies in Economic Dynamics

by

M. KALECKI

FIRST PUBLISHED IN 1943

Foreword

THESE five interconnected essays present the results of further research into the subjects which I discussed in my *Essays in the Theory of Economic Fluctuations*. In particular, more attention has been paid in the present studies to the long-run aspect of the problems considered.

Although frequent use is made of formulæ, the mathematics involved is of elementary character (elementary algebra and the beginnings of differential calculus).

The following essays are reprinted (with important alterations) by permission of the editors concerned :

" The Short-Term and the Long-Term Rate of Interest," partly from the *Review of Economic Statistics*, May 1941, partly from *Oxford Economic Papers*, No. 4 ; and " A Theory of Profits " from *Economic Journal*, June–September 1942.

I am very much indebted to Mr. F. Burchardt, Mr. J. Steindl and Mr. G. D. N. Worswick of the Oxford Institute of Statistics for valuable comments and suggestions, and to Mr. J. Goldmann for reading the proofs.

This work was started with the assistance of a grant from the National Institute of Economic and Social Research, and I take this opportunity to express due acknowledgement.

M. KALECKI.

OXFORD INSTITUTE OF STATISTICS,
November 1942.

Contents

PART ONE

Prices, Interest, and Profits

PART TWO

Business Cycle and Trend

Part One

PRICES, INTEREST, AND PROFITS

1. COSTS AND PRICES

The Percentage Gross Margins and Monopolistic Competition

1. The purpose of this essay is to discuss the relation between prime costs and prices of an industry under conditions of market imperfection and oligopoly. By an " industry " is meant here manufacturing and selling of a certain group of products which fulfils the following conditions : (i) The price fixing for a product by a firm is influenced mainly by the prices of other products in the group and the expected price reactions of firms manufacturing them, and only to a much lesser degree by prices and price reactions outside the group. (ii) The proportionate changes of the unit prime costs (unit costs of materials and wages) of the various products of an " industry " are not very divergent.

It is obvious that this definition is not clear cut. The broader the group the better condition (i) is fulfilled, and the worse in general condition (ii). The group must thus be formed so as to achieve a compromise between these two requirements and therefore the scope of the industry is within certain limits arbitrary.

Before proceeding with our discussion we shall make certain assumptions as to the average prime costs of the products in question. We assume that—as is usually the case in manufacturing—the average prime cost changes little as output expands, and that the entrepreneur takes the average prime costs as a crude approximation to the marginal costs. The latter seems to be borne out by recent inquiries which showed that entrepreneurs are really not familiar with the *exact* concept of marginal cost. In what follows we shall assume for the sake of simplicity that the average prime cost a_k of any product is *strictly* constant when output fluctuates. The marginal cost is equal to a_k and thus also

9

constant until the firm reaches its maximum capacity. At this point the marginal cost has no definite value and the price of the product is determined by the condition that output cannot be increased.

2. Imagine that in an industry a short-period equilibrium of the price system has been reached, and that no firm works up to capacity. The average prime costs of the relevant products are $a_1, a_2 \ldots a_n$. The firms fix the prices of their products, taking into consideration the mobility of customers (market imperfection) and the influence of their own prices on those of their rivals (oligopoly). Each firm is satisfied that the price p_k fixed is more advantageous than a higher or a lower level.

Imagine now that a fall in material prices and wage costs reduces all average prime costs $a_1, a_2 \ldots a_n$ in the same proportion. It will be seen that this creates for entrepreneurs an inducement to cut their prices. For the fall of average costs $a_1, a_2 \ldots a_n$ with unchanged prices $p_1, p_2 \ldots p_n$ increases the profit + overheads margins $p_k - a_k$ (we shall call them gross margins) in relation to prices p_k, and thus a cut of the price p_k by a certain percentage means a smaller percentage cut of $p_k - a_k$ than in the initial position. Consequently, if the firms stick to their previous views about what are the expected percentage increases in their sales caused by a percentage cut in prices, they must consider it profitable to reduce them. Now as long as $\dfrac{p_k - a_k}{p_k}$ remain greater than in the initial position the price fall goes on. For $p_k - a_k$ is then less affected by a given percentage cut in prices than in the initial position and, consequently, the state of affairs is more favourable for price cutting than it was before the fall of average prime costs. The price system returns to equilibrium when prices have fallen in the same proportion as average prime costs because at this point $\dfrac{p_k - a_k}{p_k}$ reach their initial level.[1]

---

[1] In terms of individual demand curves this process may be described as an iso-elastic downward shift of these curves reducing their ordinates in the proportion in which the unit prime costs have fallen.

It has been assumed throughout that the conditions of market imperfection and oligopoly were unchanged. This may, however, not be the case. Indeed, if, for instance, the market imperfection is due to transport costs and these remain unaltered while prime (production) costs decline, the fall in prices in relation to transport costs increases market imperfection. As a result prices will fall here *less* than proportionately to prime costs. For if they *did* fall proportionately to prime costs a given percentage rise in prices would increase the gross margin $p_k - a_k$ by the same percentage as in the initial position, while the expected fall in firms' sales would be smaller ; consequently the firms would consider it profitable to raise prices. Thus the increased market imperfection caused by the rise in the relation of transport costs to prime costs is here reflected in the increase of percentage gross margins $\dfrac{p_k - a_k}{p_k}$.

3. It follows from the above argument that with a given relation of average costs within the industry, and on condition that no firm is working up to capacity, the percentage gross margins $\dfrac{p_k - a_k}{p_k}$ reflect the changes in the state of market imperfection and oligopoly.

Let us now form a weighted average μ of the percentage gross margins, using as weights the respective values of sales $Q_k p_k$. We thus have

$$\mu = \frac{\Sigma Q_k p_k \dfrac{p_k - a_k}{p_k}}{\Sigma Q_k p_k} = \frac{\Sigma Q_k (p_k - a_k)}{\Sigma Q_k p_k}.$$

It may be seen at once that $\Sigma Q_k(p_k - a_k)$ represents aggregate profits + overheads of the industry, and $\Sigma Q_k p_k$ its aggregate value of sales. μ is thus equal to the ratio of profits + overheads to sales of the " industry."

We may, according to the above, say that μ reflects the changes in the degree of market imperfection and oligopoly of an industry provided : (i) the relations of average costs $a_1, a_2 \ldots a_n$ remain unchanged; (ii) no firm is working up to capacity. Thus, for instance, we may expect μ to fall when customers become more sensitive to price differences between suppliers (fall of market imperfection) and to rise when transport costs rise relative to prime production costs (rise in market imperfection, see preceding subsection). On the other hand, if technical progress reduces the average prime costs of all firms in the same proportion, it does not affect μ (unless it alters the conditions of market imperfection and oligopoly). For the argument of the preceding subsection applies whatever the cause of the fall in prime costs, provided it is uniform.

It has been stressed throughout the argument that the percentage gross margins $\dfrac{p_k - a_k}{p_k}$ reflect changes in the state of market imperfection and oligopoly only under the assumption that the ratio of prime costs $a_1, a_2 \ldots a_n$ remains unaltered. If this condition is not fulfilled $\dfrac{p_k - a_k}{p_k}$ may change, although nothing happens to alter the state of market imperfection and oligopoly. If, for instance, only the average cost a_1 falls, a_2, $a_3 \ldots a_n$ remaining unaltered, the price p_1 will be reduced for the same reason as in the case considered above when the fall in average prime costs is uniform; but in general the price p_1 will *not* fall here proportionately to a_1. For the fall of p_1 changes its relation to other prices $p_2, p_3 \ldots p_n$, and this in general affects the position with regard to the expected reaction of the sales Q_1 in response to a change in price p_1. Consequently the eventual level of $\dfrac{p_1 - a_1}{p_1}$ need not be the same as in the initial position, although no changes in conditions of market imperfection and oligopoly have occurred.[1]

---

[1] The theory of price formation when the average prime costs of firms of an " industry " do not change proportionately may be developed as follows : Let us start from a certain basic position where average prime costs are $a_1, a_2 \ldots a_n$ and prices $p_1, p_2 \ldots p_n$. Let us denote the cost and price indices in any position related to the basic position by $a'_1, a'_2 \ldots a'_n$ and $p'_1, p'_2 \ldots p'_n$ respectively. For the basic position we have thus $a'_1 = a'_2 \ldots = a'_n = 1$ and $p'_1 = p'_2 \ldots = p'_n = 1$.

It follows that the percentage gross margins $\dfrac{p_k - a_k}{p_k}$ are affected not only by changes in the state of market imperfection

Let us further denote the average of p'_k weighted according to the values of firms' sales in the basic position by $\bar{p}'$.

In accordance with the argument in the text it may be assumed that, with a given state of market imperfection and oligopoly, p'_k the price index of the firm k is a function of a'_k and $\bar{p}'$. As a first approximation we shall assume, moreover, that it is a linear function over the relevant range of changes of a'_k and $\bar{p}$, and thus we have

$$p'_k = \alpha_k a'_k + \beta_k \bar{p}' + \gamma_k. \qquad . \qquad . \qquad . \qquad (i)$$

If prime costs of all firms change in the same proportion we have $a'_k = \bar{a}'$, and it follows from the text that with a given state of market imperfection and oligopoly $p'_k = \bar{p}' = \bar{a}'$ because then all prices change in the same proportion as prime costs. It follows for this case from the above equation (i)

$$\bar{a}' = \alpha_k \bar{a}' + \beta_k \bar{a}' + \gamma_k$$

whatever the value of $\bar{a}'$, which means that provided the state of market imperfection and oligopoly does not alter,

$$\gamma_k = 0 \text{ and } \alpha_k + \beta_k = 1.$$

Consequently the equation for p'_k may be written

$$p'_k = \alpha_k a'_k + (1 - \alpha_k)\bar{p}'. \qquad . \qquad . \qquad . \qquad (ii)$$

Imagine now that a'_k increases while prime costs and prices of all other firms remain unchanged; it is then plausible to assume that p'_k increases, but in a lesser proportion than a'_k. As all prices but p'_k are assumed to be unchanged, p'_k increases in a higher proportion than $\bar{p}'$. Such a state of affairs, i.e. that p'_k increases less than a'_k but more than $\bar{p}'$, is compatible with the equation (ii) only if $a_k > 0$ and $1 - \alpha_k > 0$. It follows

$$0 < \alpha_k < 1. \qquad . \qquad . \qquad . \qquad . \qquad (iii)$$

Let us now form an average weighted according to the values of firms' sales in the basic position of both sides of equations (ii) for all firms. We obtain

$$\bar{p}' = \overline{\alpha a'} + (1 - \bar{\alpha})\bar{p}' \qquad . \qquad . \qquad . \qquad (iv)$$

where $\overline{\alpha a'}$ is the weighted average of $\alpha_k a'_k$ and $\bar{\alpha}$ the weighted average of α. Hence we obtain the formula

$$\bar{p}' = \frac{\overline{\alpha a'}}{\bar{\alpha}}. \qquad . \qquad . \qquad . \qquad . \qquad (iv')$$

After substituting this value of $\bar{p}'$ into equation (ii) we have

$$p'_k = \alpha_k a'_k + (1 - \alpha_k)\frac{\overline{\alpha a'}}{\bar{\alpha}}. \qquad . \qquad . \qquad . \qquad (ii')$$

In this way price indices of all firms are fully determined by the indices of the average prime costs a' and the coefficients α.

It may be shown that the price equilibrium determined by equations (iv') and

and oligopoly, but also by those in the relation between average prime costs $a_1, a_2 \ldots a_n$. However, the influence of these changes upon the *average* percentage gross margin μ is most probably relatively small.[1]   As further, according to our definition of industry (cf. p. 9), the relative changes in average prime costs $a_1, a_2 \ldots a_n$ are kept in rather narrow limits, it is plausible to assume that in the movement of μ there are mainly reflected

(ii) is stable. Indeed, imagine that prices deviate from the equilibrium values determined by (ii′) and as a result the average price index $\overline{p}'$ differs by Δ from the value determined by formula (iv′). It follows from the equations (ii) that this leads to price indices p'_k differing from the equilibrium level determined by the equations (ii′) by $(1 - \alpha_k) \Delta$; and from this results a new $\overline{p}'$ which differs from the equilibrium level by $(1 - \overline{\alpha})\Delta$. As according to equation (iii) $1 - \overline{\alpha} < 1$ the average price index $\overline{p}'$ will converge to its equilibrium level determined by equation (iv′).

[1] This may be corroborated by a transformation of equation (iv′) of the preceding footnote. From a known formula for the correlation coefficient it follows that

$$\overline{\alpha a}' = \overline{\alpha}\,\overline{a}' + r\sigma_\alpha \sigma_{a'}.$$

$\overline{\alpha a}'$ is the weighted average of $\alpha a'$; $\overline{\alpha}$ and $\overline{a}'$ are the weighted averages of α_k and a'_k respectively; r the coefficient of correlation between α_k and a'_k; σ_α and $\sigma_{a'}$ the standard deviations of α_k and a'_k respectively. By substituting this value of $\overline{\alpha a}'$ into equation (iv′) we obtain

$$\overline{p}' = \overline{a}' + r \frac{\sigma\alpha}{\overline{\alpha}}\sigma_{a'} \quad . \qquad . \qquad . \qquad . \qquad . \quad \text{(v)}$$

or

$$\frac{\overline{p}'}{\overline{a}'} = 1 + r \frac{\sigma_\alpha}{\overline{\alpha}} \frac{\sigma_{a'}}{\overline{a}'}. \qquad . \qquad . \qquad . \qquad . \quad \text{(v′)}$$

Now there is no particular reason for a positive or negative correlation between a'_k which is the average cost index in relation to the basic position and the coefficient α_k; thus r is likely to be rather low. If it is equal to nought $\frac{\overline{p}'}{\overline{a}'} = 1$ and then the changes in the average price $\overline{p}'$ are independent of the relative changes of average prime costs a: the average price index $\overline{p}'$ is equal to the average prime cost index $\overline{a}'$.

In general, of course, r is not equal to zero. But it is likely to be lower in absolute value than, say, 0.30; further, even assuming a very wide dispersion in the coefficients α_k it is unlikely that $\frac{\sigma_\alpha}{\overline{\alpha}}$ would be higher than, say, 0.5. On these assumptions the absolute value of $r\frac{\sigma_\alpha}{\overline{\alpha}} \frac{\sigma_{a'}}{\overline{a}'} < 0.15 \frac{\sigma_{a'}}{\overline{a}'}$, and thus

$$1 - 0.15 \frac{\sigma_{a'}}{\overline{a}'} < \frac{\overline{p}'}{\overline{a}'} < 1 + 0.15 \frac{\sigma_{a'}}{\overline{a}'}.$$

changes in the degree of market imperfection and oligopoly. This, however, is still subject to the qualification that the firms do not work up to capacity.

4. Let us start from a position for which this condition is fulfilled and imagine that the effective demand for the products of the " industry " increases. As long as firms do not reach the point of full capacity the percentage gross margins remain unaltered unless the rise in demand has some effect upon the state of market imperfection and oligopoly.[1] If, however, the increase in demand continues, one firm after another will reach its maximum capacity beyond which it is unable to increase its output. It is obvious that if the demand for the firm's product rises while the supply is limited by the existing capacity, the prices charged by the firm will increase so as to bring into equilibrium the increased demand with the fixed supply—even though the average prime costs and the state of market imperfection and oligopoly are unaltered. This will result in the increase of the average percentage gross margin μ. We may thus conclude that in the movement of μ are mainly reflected changes in the degree of market imperfection and oligopoly and bottlenecks in the manufacturing of the products of the " industry," appearing as the demand for these products increases in relation to available capacities.

5. In all the above argument we have abstracted from selling costs and we must now allow for them. It may be assumed that the entrepreneur apportions a certain part of his selling costs to " investment or overhead selling costs " (a considerable part of advertisement is probably treated in this way) and the rest to " prime selling costs." The first may be included in overheads and profits while the second plays in price formation a rôle similar to prime production costs.

The entrepreneur may now be imagined to fix his price on the assumption that it is profitable for him to spend a certain percentage of the proceeds σ on prime selling costs. σ may be called the rate of prime selling costs. It is easy to see that in

---

[1] In terms of individual demand curves this means an iso-elastic shift of these curves to the right.

our argument on pages 10-11, attempting to establish that (with qualifications stated there) in the movement of $\dfrac{p_k - a_k}{p_k}$ are reflected changes in the state of market imperfection and oligopoly, $\dfrac{p_k - a_k}{p_k}$ must now be replaced by $\dfrac{p_k - a_k}{p_k} - \sigma$. It follows that if selling costs are allowed for, the average percentage gross margin μ reflects not only the changes in the degree of market imperfection and oligopoly and the bottlenecks in available capacities, but also changes in the rates of prime selling costs.

To summarise : in the movement of the average percentage gross margin μ are mainly reflected changes in the degree of market imperfection and oligopoly, changes in the rates of prime selling costs, and bottlenecks in available manufacturing capacities. (To a minor degree μ is influenced also by changes in the relation of prime production costs $a_1, a_2 \ldots a_n$ within the "industry.")

6. As shown on page 11, the ratio of profits + overheads to proceeds is equal to the average percentage gross margin μ. It is easy to see that μ determines the distribution of the net output (or value added) between wages on the one hand and profits + overheads on the other, if in addition the ratio of the cost of materials to that of wages is given. If we denote the wage bill by W and the ratio of the material bill to the wage bill by m, the aggregate prime costs are $(1 + m)W$. As the ratio of overheads + profits to proceeds $= \mu$, the ratio of overheads + profits to prime costs $= \dfrac{\mu}{1 - \mu}$. It follows that overheads + profits $= \dfrac{\mu}{1 - \mu}(1 + m)W$. Further, the net output (or value added) is equal to the sum of overheads + profits and the wage bill, and thus we have

$$\text{net output} = \frac{\mu}{1 - \mu}(1 + m)W + W.$$

Thus the relative share of wages w in the net output is

$$w = \frac{W}{\dfrac{\mu}{1-\mu}(1+m)W + W} = \frac{1-\mu}{1+\mu m}.$$

It may be seen at once that w is a diminishing function of both μ and m. That means that if, e.g., a change in the state of imperfect competition and oligopoly, in the rates of prime selling costs or in the "bottleneck factors" presses down the ratio of overheads + profits to proceeds μ, it tends to increase the relative share of wages in the net output w. But apart from this w depends on the ratio of material costs to wage costs m : it falls when the cost of materials rises in relation to that of wages and conversely.

Changes in the Percentage Gross Margin of an Industry

1. It has been shown above that changes in the average percentage gross margin of an "industry," i.e. of the ratio of its overheads + profits to its proceeds μ, are determined chiefly by changes in the state of market imperfection and oligopoly, changes in the rate of prime selling costs, and by the bottleneck factors. It is proposed to examine in this section how μ is affected through these channels by the business cycle and the long-run economic development. We shall deal first with the business cycle.

2. If market imperfection depends partly on transport costs, and the average prime costs a_k fall while transport costs remain unchanged or fall in a lesser proportion, the market imperfection and consequently the average percentage gross margin μ increases.[1]

Now it is a rather frequent case that prime production costs fall more strongly than transport costs in the slump. Thus under this influence μ will tend to rise in the slump and to fall in the boom.

There exists, however, a reason for cyclical changes in market imperfection, and thus in μ in the opposite direction, which has been indicated by Mr. Harrod. He calls attention to the fact

---

[1] Cf. p. 11.

that buyers are more careful in comparing prices charged by various sellers in the slump than in the boom. This would tend to cause a fall in market imperfection and the gross profit percentage margin μ in the slump and its rise in the boom. It should be added perhaps that if the slump is deep the market imperfection is likely to be relatively low in the subsequent recovery also, because the habit of more careful buying acquired during depression may persist for a certain time.

Probably more important than the effect of cyclical changes in market imperfection upon μ is the influence of " tacit agreements " in a deep slump which may be classified as changes in the degree of oligopoly.

Imagine a deep slump in which the average prime costs in an " industry " have fallen considerably. If the percentage margins were unchanged there would be an even stronger fall of what is left for overheads and profits of a single producer because output is reduced as well. The resulting deterioration in his financial position induces him to increase his percentage gross margin in the hope that other producers will act likewise. If they do not he is lost, but so he would be if he reduced his prices proportionately to average prime costs. If such is the prevailing attitude, a " tacit agreement " is established and μ is higher than it otherwise would be.

It is important to note that the rise in a percentage gross margin does not mean here a high measure of profit because it only compensates partly for the fall in average prime costs and output. The existing firms need not be afraid therefore that new enterprises will emerge; and even many " high cost producers " must close down in spite of the " tacit agreement."

When the slump is over, the degree of oligopoly will fall for various reasons. First, the rise in average prime costs and output removes the very basis of the tacit agreement, the more so that in the meantime a certain cut in " overhead expenditure " has probably been achieved; second, because of the fear of newcomers, and even more so to prevent the reopening of establishments closed down in the slump.

On the basis of the above analysis it seems probable that in a cycle showing no deep and prolonged slumps the changes of μ caused by fluctuations in the state of market imperfection and oligopoly or in prime selling costs are not likely to be important.

The position will be different in a deep and prolonged slump and also in the subsequent recovery. The most important factor in the slump is likely to be then the " tacit agreement " and thus μ may rise significantly. On the other hand, in the subsequent recovery μ is likely to fall below what would be its level after a moderate slump. Two factors will contribute to it : the " careful buying " which persists for a certain time after a deep and prolonged slump, and the tendency of the entrepreneurs to prevent reopening of numerous establishments closed down in the slump.

3. We have yet to deal with the influence upon the percentage gross margin of the " bottleneck factors " which come into the picture when the volume of sales of an " industry " increases in relation to its capacity beyond a certain point. The resulting rise in the percentage gross margin is likely to be significant only close to the top of the boom when the utilization of equipment is high. And in the light of the data we give in the next section it does not seem usually important even then for manufacturing industry as a whole. (It must be noted, however, that these data relate to the twentieth century only.)

It looks as if the influence of bottlenecks in manufacturing in a modern capitalist society becomes predominant only in " abnormal " times, during wars or after-war periods. In such periods total employment, and, consequently, the wage bill, expressed in terms of wage units, remains unaltered or even increases. At the same time the production of consumption goods is strongly curtailed, chiefly owing to the scarcity of raw materials and labour in the industries concerned. As a result, if the consumption of non-wage earners is not reduced sufficiently by increased propensity to save, taxation, and rationing to offset this divergency, prices will rise in relation to wage rates, i.e. the real wage rate will fall. This may happen in two ways : by the increase in prices of raw materials relative to wage rates and by the rise in the percentage gross margins of the manufactured products.   Usually both these changes go hand in hand, although, if prices of raw materials are controlled and they are distributed among enterprises by a quota system, the equilibrium between demand for and supply of consumption goods is achieved only by the rise in percentage gross margins.   The rise in money wage rates enforced by the workers who try to restore the " old " real wages cannot remedy the situation, and results only in a new rise in prices ; for at the root of the trouble lies the fall in the ratio of production of consumption goods to total employment.   It is this that is the actual cause of the " vicious spiral."

The position in an " ordinary " boom is different in that bottlenecks in plant and labour are not very significant.   True, the supply of basic raw materials is sometimes inelastic and their prices increase considerably in relation to wage rates.   This, however, results only in a rather slight increase in the prices of finished goods relative to wage rates because, usually, the basic raw materials are a much smaller cost item than wages.   And even this tendency of real wages to fall is often counterbalanced (1) by the institutional rigidity of certain items in the cost of living (rents, bus and railway fares, etc.), which often causes their fall relative to wage rates when these increase, and (2) by technical progress which reduces the labour cost per unit of product relative to wage rates.   As a result the fall in real wage rates in an " ordinary " recovery is small if any, and does not initiate, therefore, a " vicious spiral."

4. We shall now consider briefly the influence of long-run economic development upon the percentage gross margin μ.

As to the imperfection of the market, it will tend to diminish as a result of the fall of transport costs in relation to prime production costs, standardization of goods, spreading of commodity exchanges, etc. ; the higher standard of living may tend to cause less careful buying (the " Harrodian factor "), but this will probably be fully offset by a higher degree of knowledge and more free time for buying ; finally, at a certain late stage of capitalist development the expansion of advertisement may in many cases create an " artificial " market imperfection.   With regard to oligopoly, the progressive concentration of industry is likely to enhance its degree. The rates of prime selling cost are also likely to rise in the long run, particularly at a certain late stage of capitalist development.

As to the influence of "bottleneck factors," it seems that at least in the twentieth century they are effective in "normal times" only close to the top of the boom and even then are not very significant for manufacturing industry as a whole. Thus "bottleneck factors" are probably not important in the long-run analysis of recent economic developments. This does not, however, exclude a possibility of significant long-run changes in μ caused by these factors.[1]

On balance it is impossible to say *a priori* how μ changes in the long run. But it follows clearly from the above that (if we abstract from bottleneck factors) it is more likely to rise in the later than in the earlier stage of capitalist development.

Application to the U.S.A. Manufacturing Industry

1. Apart from the causes of changes in the percentage gross margin of an "industry" discussed in the preceding section, there will be a variety of other factors influencing it. However, the above analysis gives a more or less comprehensive list of important factors which affect the gross profit percentage margins of *all* industries simultaneously as a result of the business cycle or long-run economic development. If we consider the percentage gross margin of the manufacturing industry as a whole (i.e. the ratio of its aggregate overheads + profits to its aggregate proceeds), it is these influences that will be most important while particular factors affecting percentage gross margins of thousands of industries will most probably cancel out. We therefore apply the results of the preceding discussion to the U.S.A. manufacturing industry as a whole.

Two problems arise here, however. The first depends on the existence of industries which are dominated by one firm or a cartel. To such a case our analysis, which was concerned with

---

[1] Cf. p. 30, below.

an industry working in conditions of imperfect competition and oligopoly, does not apply. It may be said, however, (i) that the predominant form of a manufacturing industry *is* that working under conditions of imperfect competition and oligopoly, (ii) that even " pure monopolists " must count with potential outsiders and this makes their behaviour broadly similar to that of oligopolies. It is therefore likely that the existence of cartels, etc., does not invalidate the application of the apparatus built up above for the examination of the percentage gross margin of the U.S.A. manufacturing industry as a whole.

The second difficulty is that changes in the ratio of aggregate overheads + profits of manufacturing industry to its aggregate proceeds are influenced not only by changes in such ratios of the particular industries but also by changes in the proportions of proceeds of these industries ; indeed μ may have different values for various industries and thus, for instance, the increased weight for industries with high μ may increase the ratio of overheads + profits to proceeds for the manufacturing industry as a whole although such ratios for the component industries have not changed. As far, however, as it could be ascertained by considering the changes of μ for industrial groups, this influence upon μ of the U.S.A. manufacturing industry as a whole was of no importance.

2. We give below the ratio of overheads + profits of the U.S.A. manufacturing industry to its proceeds in the period 1899-1937, calculated from the Census of Manufactures.[1]

[1] As given in the *Statistical Abstract of the United States*, 1939. To make, however, the figures for various years comparable, the following adjustments had to be made : (1) Prior to 1931 the tax on tobacco manufactures has been deducted from overheads + profits, where it was included by the Census. (ii) Prior to 1935 the cost of work given out has been subtracted from overheads + profits, where it was included by the Census. Up to 1923 this has been done according to Census data ; from then onwards the percentage of the cost of work given out in terms of total prime costs has been assumed the same as in 1923. (iii) In 1929, 1931 and 1933, in which years the work and shop supplies were included by the Census in overheads + profits as opposed to other years, a corresponding correction has been introduced. In 1904 the work and shop supplies were—according to the Census data—0·7 per cent. of total prime costs. In accordance with the rise of the value of capital equipment taken from Professor Douglas, *The Theory of*

TABLE I

The Percentage Gross Margin μ in the U.S.A. Manufacturing Industry

	%		%		%
1899	23·1	1919	22·4	1929	26·7
1904	23·3	1921	21·9	1931	28·1
1909	23·3	1923	23·2	1933	27·9
1914	22·5	1925	24·2	1935	25·0
		1927	25·3	1937	24·8

Figure 1 represents the time curve of μ. It may be seen at once that in the period 1899-1929 all points of it lie on a smooth

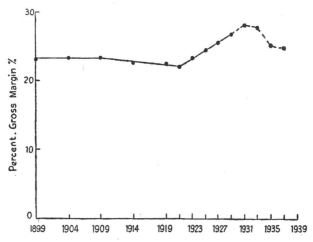

FIG. 1.—Percentage Gross Margin of U.S. Manufacturing Industry, 1899-1937.

curve formed by three straight lines : 1899-1909, 1909-21, and 1921-29. This may be interpreted as showing the absence of any business cycle effects upon μ, inclusive of the influence of " bottleneck factors." The long-period trend of μ, as repre-sented by the curve 1899-1909-21-29 shows stability of μ in the period 1899-1909 and a slow fall in 1909-21. This may be accounted for as a balance between conflicting tendencies, described in the last section (pp. 20-21). We see then a rather

Wages, as compared with the value of prime costs, this percentage has been assumed 1 per cent for the years 1929, 1931 and 1933. (iv) The change in the scope of the Census in 1914 is accounted for by linking up the series.

sharp rise in μ in the period 1921-29. This is probably caused by what may be called a " commercial revolution " which took place in that period. The violent development of modern selling methods (advertisement, " invention " of new products, etc.) caused both an increase in prime selling costs and created an " artificial " market imperfection.

The changes of μ in the period 1929-37 show quite a different pattern from those in the period 1899-1929. While cyclical changes were not noticeable in the latter period, after 1929 we see a strong increase in μ in the slump (1931, 1933) and a still stronger fall in the subsequent recovery (1935, 1937). This may be explained by the effects of a deep and prolonged slump as described in the preceding section : " tacit agreement " in the slump, and in the recovery its reversal strengthened by the tendency to prevent the reopening of establishments closed down in the slump and by the habit of " careful buying " persisting for a certain time as an after-effect of the slump.

In this connection it is interesting to notice that changes in the percentage gross margins μ (i.e. the ratios of overheads + profits to proceeds) in the wholesale and retail trade in the U.S.A. show a similar pattern as in manufacturing in the period 1929-37.

TABLE II

The Percentage Gross Margin μ in Manufacturing Industry, Wholesale Trade, and Retail Trade in the U.S.A.

Year.	Manufacturing. Industry.[1]	Wholesale Trade.[2]	Retail Trade.[2]
	%	%	%
1929	26·7	14·3	29·6
1931	28·1	15·0	30·9
1933	27·9	15·2	32·8
1935	25·0	12·5	29·0
1937	24·8	12·9	28·7

[1] Taken from Table I.

[2] Difference between sales and purchase costs of goods sold expressed as a percentage of sales. Thus prime costs are here identified with purchase costs of goods, which is approximately correct. Source, B. M. Fowler and W. H. Shaw, " Distributive Costs of Consumption Goods," *Survey of Current Business*, July 1942. The figures relate to wholesale and retail trade in consumption goods only.

The above cannot, of course, provide a full proof of the correctness of our theory. It shows only that this can supply a plausible interpretation of changes in pricing in the U.S.A. manufacturing industries (and wholesale and retail trade in that country in the period 1929-37). It will therefore be useful to examine to what extent the alternative theories of price formation are capable of explaining the phenomena in question.

3. We may distinguish two theories of price formation alternative to ours : (i) the perfect competition theory, (ii) the " full cost " theory.

The supporters of the perfect competition theory do not deny in fact the existence of market imperfection and oligopoly. But they consider them to be factors of minor importance and thus maintain that the assumption of perfect competition is justified to the first approximation.[1]

One of the important corollaries of the free competition theory is that the relative share of wages in the value added (net output) falls in the boom and rises in the slump. Indeed, price being equal to short-period marginal costs, the average value added (i.e. price — average cost of materials) is approximately equal to the marginal wage cost, since it may be assumed that the average cost of materials is independent of the firm's output and the marginal cost of salaries and depreciation is small. Further, under perfect competition the relevant branch of the marginal wage cost curve is upward sloping ; also the average wage cost increases from a point onwards but (unless the shape of its curve is very peculiar) it increases in a smaller proportion than the marginal wage cost ; so that the ratio of average to marginal wage cost falls when the utilization of plant increases. It follows

---

[1] Cf., for instance, J. R. Hicks, *Value and Capital* : " If we can suppose that the percentages by which prices exceed marginal costs are neither very large nor very variable, and if we can suppose (what is largely the consequence of the first assumption) that *marginal* costs do generally increase with output at the point of equilibrium (diminishing marginal costs being rare), then the laws of an economic system, working under perfect competition, will not be appreciably varied in a system which contains widespread elements of monopoly " (p. 84). The only justification of these assumptions is that " a universal adoption of the assumption of monopoly must have very destructive consequences for economic theory " (p. 83).

directly that the relative share of wages in the value added falls in the boom when the utilization of the plant increases, and rises in the slump when the utilization of the plant diminishes. This consequence of free competition theory may be tested by statistical data. In Table III we give the relative share of wages w in the value added for the U.S.A. manufacturing industry in the period 1919-37.[1]

TABLE III

The Relative Share of Wages w in the Value Added by the U.S.A. Manufacturing Industry

	%		%
1919	41·8	1929	37·5
1921	45·0	1931	37·4
1923	42·9	1933	36·7
1925	40·4	1935	39·4
1927	39·8	1937	40·2

The only instance when the theory accords with fact is the slump year 1921, when the relative share of wages in the value added is higher than in 1919 and 1923. It falls, however, after 1923 in 1925 and 1927, although in both these years the degree of utilization of equipment was definitely lower than in 1923. (1923 was the year of highest degree of utilization in the period 1921-37.) Further, in the slump years 1931 and 1933 w remains at the level of the boom year 1929 and rises in the subsequent recovery in 1935 and 1937. Thus the facts are rather against the perfect competition theory.

It should be added that changes in the relative share of wages in the value added w are fully determined by those in the gross profit percentage margin μ and the ratio of the material bill to the wage bill m (see p. 17). Thus if the above interpretation (pp. 23-24) of changes in μ in the U.S.A. manufacturing in terms of our theory is accepted, this theory provides *eo ipso* an explanation for changes in w.

[1] Based on the data of " Census of Manufactures," as given in the *Statistical Abstract of the U.S.A.*, 1939, with the same adjustments as described in the footnote to p. 22. The comparable figures for the period 1899-1914 are :

1899	42·7	1909	41·0
1904	42·5	1914	42·1

4. The full cost theory in its familiar version maintains that the firm fixes its price by adding to average prime cost the overheads per unit of actual output or per unit of " standard " output (i.e. per unit of output corresponding to what is considered reasonably full employment of firms' plant) and " something " for profit. This statement has no precise theoretical meaning because the amount that is added for profit makes quite a lot of difference to the price and more still to the gross margin.

The full cost theory has been actually derived from the replies of entrepreneurs to the inquiries about their pricing methods.[1] But it is not unlikely that the procedure described by them is not the actual process of fixing prices but only a check applied to prices fixed in another way to see whether they make any net profit. Indeed, if the " something " which is the difference between price and the full cost calculated per unit of actual output is positive the firm knows that it makes a net profit on the product in question. If overheads are calculated per unit of " standard " output the positive difference means that losses if any are due to the fall in output only, and if the slump is not too deep and prolonged they have no importance from a longer point of view; while if the slump *is* deep and prolonged the " standard " output is being appropriately reduced. Both in the case of calculation with actual and with " standard " output the calculator seems not so much to fix the price as to translate the price fixed by other considerations into the " full cost language." In a modern cotton spinning mill the manager described once to me at great length the work of their calculating department. To my question, however, how the results are used to fix the prices, he replied : " Oh, the prices are fixed by the market."

Nevertheless, in certain circumstances the calculator's analysis may have some bearing upon fixing of prices. In a deep slump it helps to realize the precarious position of the firm and thereby it initiates the attempts to increase the percentage gross margin, and so may lead to the establishment of a " tacit agreement."

[1] See, for instance, R. L. Hall and C. J. Hitch, " Price Theory and Business Behaviour," *Oxford Economic Papers*, May 1939.

Percentage Gross Margin and Capital Intensity

1. We have shown in the preceding sections that both short-term and long-term changes in the ratio of overheads + profits to proceeds μ are determined chiefly by changes in the state of market imperfection and oligopoly by changes in the rates of prime selling costs, and by "bottleneck factors." True, μ is influenced also by relative changes in the average prime costs as between firms, but this influence is likely to be not very important. It follows that if in the long run the state of market imperfection and oligopoly and the rates of prime selling costs remain stable and "bottleneck factors" do not come into the picture, the ratio of profits + overheads to proceeds μ is more or less constant.

This is in contradiction with the widely accepted view that in the long run the relative share of overheads and profits in the price increases owing to the rising capital intensity of production. We must therefore analyse the basis of this contention and then examine also what effect the increase of capital intensity has upon the percentage gross margin according to our theory.

2. The argument in favour of μ rising with capital intensity of production runs roughly as follows. As a result of technical progress more capital is used per unit of output, and therefore the value of capital (at reproduction prices) rises relatively to the value of production. Now the rate of depreciation being stable or increasing, and the rate of profit more or less stable, profit + depreciation, must rise in relation to the value of production. The salary bill usually rises with capital intensity in relation to wage bill + material bill. Hence the relative share of overheads +profits in the value of production μ must be expected to increase. Two objections may be raised, however, against this argument.

First, the assumption that the rate of profit in the long run is rather stable is, in fact, quite arbitrary. It is based on the idea that the rate of profit in long periods tends to be equal to the long-term rate of interest + "normal profit" and that both these components change rather slowly. But this long period equilibrium approach is not justified because the long-run economic development is a complicated dynamic process, and the rate of profit may very well fall in the long run, although the long-term rate of interest remains constant (or even increases).[1] Thus the ratio of overheads + profits to proceeds may remain constant in spite of the fall of the value of production in relation to the value of capital. A striking example of such a situation is provided by the developments in the U.S.A. manufacturing industry in the period 1899-1914:

TABLE IV

The Ratio of the Value of Production to the Value of Capital and the Percentage Gross Margin in the U.S.A. Manufacturing Industry

Year.	(1) Reproduction Cost of Fixed Capital.[2]	(2) Value of Products.[3]	(3) Ratio (2):(1).	(4) Long-Term Rate of Interest.[4]	(5) Percentage Gross Margin μ.[5]
	(1899 = 100)			%	%
1899	100	100	100	3·1	23·1
1904	137	130	95	3·5	23·3
1909	216	182	84	3·6	23·3
1914	280	212	76	4·0	22·5

There is, however, still another objection against the argument on which the statement is based that the percentage gross margin μ increases with capital intensity of production. The rise in the latter means that capital contained in equipment increases relative to its maximum productive capacity. The ratio of actual output to capital depends in addition on the degree of

[1] The determinants of the rate of profit are discussed below in the essay " A Theory of Profits."

[2] Obtained by multiplying the index of real fixed capital by the price index of investment goods. Both series are taken from Professor Douglas, *The Theory of Wages*, p. 121. Douglas' series extends to 1922, but his post-war figures are not quite reliable because he did not take into account the possible revaluation of capital by firms in connection with the " price revolution." I am indebted for this point to Mr. E. Rothbarth.

[3] Taken from the " Census of Manufactures " (the changes in the scope of the Census in 1914 are accounted for by linking up the series).

[4] Douglas, *op. cit.*, p. 469. [5] Cf. p. 23.

2

utilization of equipment, i.e. the ratio of actual output to maximum capacity. If, therefore, the rise in capital intensity is accompanied by an increase in the degree of utilization, the value of production does not necessarily fall relative to the value of capital.

It follows that rising capital intensity, even if the rate of profit remains stable, is compatible with a constant percentage gross margin μ : the rise in the degree of utilization of equipment may offset the influence of the increase in capital intensity. It should be noticed, however, that if this increase lasts for a certain time there will be reached a point of the degree of utilization where " bottleneck factors " appear and then μ starts to rise.

We may thus formulate the interrelation between μ and the rise in capital intensity according to our theory as follows : Let us start from a situation where " bottleneck factors " are absent, and thus μ is determined by the state of market imperfection and oligopoly (and by the rates of prime selling costs). If there is a rise in capital intensity of production and the degree of utilization does not increase, the rate of profit falls, while the percentage gross margin is stable.[1] If, however, the degree of utilization increases sufficiently to offset the influence of increased capital intensity, the rate of profit can be maintained ; and if the rise in the utilization of equipment has not brought " bottleneck factors " into the picture the percentage gross margin is also stable here. But if this development—rising intensity of capital, stable rate of profit, rising utilization of equipment—continues for some time, a point will be reached where bottlenecks do appear. It is only after this stage has been reached that increasing capital intensity must cause either a fall of the rate of profit or a rise in the percentage gross margin.

3. On page 17 we have deduced the following formula for the relative share of wages in the value added by manufacturing :

$$w = \frac{1 - \mu}{1 + \mu m}$$

[1] This situation corresponds roughly to that assumed by Marx in his law of the falling rate of profit.

where μ is the percentage gross margin and m the ratio of the material bill to the wage bill. Now, as long as " bottleneck factors " do not come into the picture changes in μ depend chiefly on changes in the state of market imperfection and oligopoly (and in the rates of prime selling costs). Thus if these determinants are unchanged technical progress can affect w only by influencing the ratio of the material bill to the wage bill. A fall in the wage cost, for instance, in relation to the raw material cost will raise m and thus reduce the relative share of wages in the value added. But if technical progress reduces in the same proportion the cost of labour and the prices of raw materials, w remains unchanged—provided that " bottleneck factors " do not cause any change in μ.

2. THE SHORT-TERM AND THE LONG-TERM RATE OF INTEREST

The Short-Term Rate

1. Before we discuss the problem of the formation of the short-term rate of interest it is necessary to establish first a functional connection between the short-term rate of interest and the velocity of cash circulation. By the latter we mean the ratio of turnover, T, to the stock of cash (current accounts or notes), M. It is clear that the smaller, with a given turnover, is the amount of cash possessed, say, by a firm, the greater the convenience derived from the marginal unit of cash in managing transactions. Moreover, after cash holding is reduced to a certain level, its further curtailment involves a very strongly rising marginal inconvenience. On the other hand, if cash is very plentiful with a given turnover, the marginal convenience falls to nought and remains at this level if the amount of cash, M, increases further. The marginal convenience of holding cash, therefore, is an increasing function of the velocity of circulation, T/M, and may be represented by a J curve.

The short-term rate of interest is closely connected with the marginal convenience of holding cash. Indeed, if the short-term rate is higher than this marginal convenience, there is an inducement for lending additional cash; if the short-term rate is lower, it becomes profitable to withdraw from short-term assets and acquire cash. Thus equilibrium is reached when the short-term rate of interest is equal to the marginal convenience of holding cash.

The above requires a certain qualification. The operation of short-term lending as such involves some costs and inconveniences, or "investment costs." The short-term rate is thus equal to the sum of the marginal convenience of holding cash + "investment costs." Thus when the marginal convenience of cash holding falls to nought the short-term rate is equal to investment costs.   As a result we may say that *a priori* grounds exist for postulating a connection between the short-term rate and the velocity of circulation of the shape represented by the curve in Figure 2.[1]   That this curve must not be assumed to be absolutely stationary through time is obvious.   Habits of cash holding, etc., may change in the long run, and a financial panic may cause

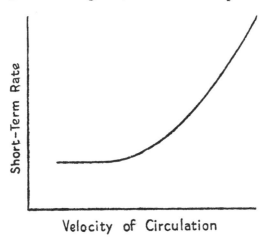

FIG. 2.—Hypothetical Relationship between Velocity of Circulation and the Short-Term Rate of Interest.

higher requirements for cash at the same turnover and the same short-term rate ; this will be reflected in a shift of the curve.

2. We shall now try to verify statistically the relationship under consideration.   Since 1930 the London Clearing Banks have published figures of turnover (debit entries to current accounts).   The ratio of these figures to current accounts may

[1] There arises here the problem whether in this context the short-term rate of interest must be understood gross or net of income tax.   If the marginal inconvenience of curtailment of the cash holding is supposed by a manager to be finally reflected in a corresponding reduction of profits, then it is the interest gross of tax which should be taken into account.   This seems likely to be the case.   However, the subsequent empirical inquiry which relates to the U.K. in the period 1930-38 is independent of this assumption because the rate of income tax was fairly stable over that period.

seem to be just what we need for our investigation, but unfortunately the case is not so simple.

The turnover consists of two parts, each of a very different character : of financial and of non-financial transactions. For 1930 the latter were estimated to have constituted only 15 per cent of the total turnover.[1] On the other hand, the financial current accounts are unlikely to be more than one-third of the total.[2] This disproportion reflects the obvious fact of the much greater velocity of circulation of financial, compared with non-financial, accounts. As a result changes in the velocity of circulation of financial accounts are reflected in the ratio of turnover to current accounts too heavily in relation to the share of financial accounts in the latter. This defect can be remedied in the following way. We divide the turnover into the non-financial and financial components ; we reduce the financial component in a proportion which brings its ratio to financial accounts in the base year 1930 to the level of the ratio of the non-financial component to non-financial accounts, i.e. to the level of the non-financial velocity of circulation. Finally, we add the " reduced financial component " to the non-financial component and divide the sum by total current accounts. This ratio may be considered an adequate index of changes in the velocity of circulation.

The calculation is described in detail in my paper on " The Short-Term Rate of Interest and the Velocity of Circulation." [3] The results obtained there [4] are given in Table V and plotted in Figure 3.

As we see, all points except 1931 lie around a curve of a shape which we deduced on *a priori* grounds in the preceding paragraph. Point 1931 is considerably above the curve. This is explained by the financial crisis in the second half of that year which caused

[1] E. H. Phelps Brown and G. L. S. Shackle, *Statistics of Monetary Circulation in England and Wales, 1919-1937* (Royal Economic Society, Memorandum No. 74), p. 28.

[2] *Ibid.*, p. 33.   [3] *Review of Economic Statistics*, May 1941.

[4] Slightly revised ; allowance having been made for : (1) a change in the working practice of Town Clearings in November 1932 which increased the volume of total clearings by about 2 per cent ; (2) a change in the scope of current accounts in January 1938 which caused an increase by about 2 per cent.

TABLE V

Index of Velocity of Circulation and Rate on Treasury Bills

Year.	Velocity of Circulation (1930 = 100).	Rate on Treasury Bills (%).
1930	100	2·48
1931	95	3·59
1932	93	1·49
1933	83	0·59
1934	88	0·73
1935	85	0·55
1936	82	0·58
1937	84	0·56
1938	80	0·61

an upward shift of the curve considered, i.e. increased the amount of cash required at a given turnover and a given short-term rate

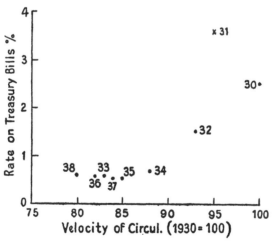

FIG. 3.—Velocity of Circulation and Rate on Treasury Bills, 1930-38.

of interest.[1]   The period examined is rather short, and further inquiries are necessary to confirm the theory.

[1] The point for the year 1938 is also slightly raised by the increase of the short-term rate in the autumn, due to political events.

3. The relation examined above may be written

$$T/M = V(\rho) \qquad . \qquad . \qquad . \qquad . \qquad (1)$$

where T is the money volume of transactions (turnover), M the stock of cash and $V(\rho)$ the velocity of circulation, being an increasing function of the short-term rate of interest ρ. Formula (1) may also be written

$$M V(\rho) = T. \qquad . \qquad . \qquad . \qquad (1a)$$

In this form it is nothing else but the quantity of money equation.[1] The significance of it is, however, quite different here than in the quantity theory of money. It shows simply that with a *given* volume of transactions T an increase in the supply of cash M by the banking system causes a fall in the short-term rate of interest. One can, of course, argue that this fall tends to increase the rate of investment, and thus through this channel it influences T. But, as we shall see in the following sections of this essay, changes in the short-term rate have a rather small immediate effect upon the long-term rate ; and it is chiefly the latter which is relevant for investment activity. Thus, only after the new level of the short-term rate of interest has been maintained for a rather prolonged time will it affect appreciably the rate of investment. Therefore the *immediate* influence of the increase in the supply of cash will be not to raise the money volume of transactions but to reduce the velocity of circulation and the short-term rate of interest.

4. It is still interesting to discuss the mechanism of the increase in the supply of current accounts by the banking system. Imagine that banks decide to reduce their cash ratio (the ratio of the amount of their notes and accounts in the Central Bank to deposits, i.e. current and deposit accounts) and buy bills. Let us first assume that the rate on deposit accounts follows the discount rate. Thus when the discount rate starts to fall there will be no inducement to sell bills and open deposit accounts instead. The rate of discount must consequently fall to such a level at

---

[1] T is the *money* volume of transactions and thus stands for PT in the Fisher equation.

which people will be prepared to add to their current accounts the amount for which the banks buy bills. With a given turn-over T_0 this level of the short-term rate may be obtained easily by means of formula (1a). Indeed, if the initial state of current accounts is M_0 and the banks bought bills for the amount B, then

$$(M_0 + B)V(\rho) = T_0.$$

If the rate on deposit accounts remains unchanged, the process is more complicated. For a fall in the discount rate then induces some people to sell bills and acquire deposit accounts. The fall in the discount rate is therefore smaller than in the case previously considered: it will fall to the level at which the sum of the increases in current *and* deposit accounts is equal to the amount B of bills bought by the banks.

The Short-Term Rate and the Long-Term Rate

1. It has been shown in the preceding section that the short-term rate of interest is determined by the volume of transactions and the supply of cash by the banking system. We shall now examine the problem of the determination of the long-term rate.

In order to establish a connection between the short-term and the long-term rate, we shall examine the problem of substitution between a representative short-term asset, say a bill of exchange, and a representative long-term asset, say a Consol. Imagine a person or enterprise considering how to invest its reserves. It will be, I think, a frequent case that the security holder compares the result of holding one or the other type of security over a few years. Thus in comparing the yields he takes into account the expected average discount rate over this period, which we denote by ρ_e and the present long-term rate (yield of Consols) r. We must now consider the advantages and disadvantages of both types of securities which account for the difference $r - \rho_e$.

There is first to be considered the possibility of a capital loss if at some time Consols will have to be converted into cash. It should be taken into account, however, that the holder need not actually sell bonds in order to obtain the cash required: he may

2 *

take bank credits against their security up to a high percentage of their value.[1] There still remains the disadvantage, as compared with bills, that this percentage is less than 100 per cent and that the interest on such credits is slightly higher than the rate of discount. (When the holder converts bills into cash his income is reduced by the interest which the bills yield ; when he borrows against the security of bonds, by the interest he pays on bank credit.) On the other hand, the holding of bills which must be re-bought every three months involves various inconveniences and costs, and this often causes money to be invested on short term not in bills but in loans to the discount market.[2] If, therefore, we denote by β the value corresponding to the net disadvantages of bond holding from this point of view, it follows from the above that β is not necessarily positive and that it is normally small, say of the order of $\frac{1}{2}$ per cent.[3]

There is, however, yet another more important factor contributing to the difference $r - \rho_e$. The holding of bills guarantees the integrity of the principal. On the other hand, bonds may depreciate during the period for which the results of investment are considered. Short-period fluctuations of the value of securities owned may be disregarded [4] by the holder, but if the capital loss proves to have a permanent character it must be reckoned as such. Therefore a provision for the risk of depreciation γ must be taken into account when the yields r and ρ_e are compared. We thus have

$$r - \rho_e = \beta + \gamma. \qquad . \qquad . \qquad . \quad (2)$$

[1] I am indebted for this point to Mr. P. W. S. Andrews.

[2] In other words, "costs of investment" in bills (cf. p. 32) are relatively high.

[3] The margin between the rate on loans to the discount market and the discount rate is, say, $\frac{1}{2}$-1 per cent ; that between discount rate and the rate on credits against the security of bonds, say, 1-2 per cent. It does not, however, follow that β is necessarily, or even normally, positive ; because the latter margin, unlike the first, applies only to the periods during which the purchaser expects to be using his assets to obtain cash. β may therefore be regarded as tending to equal a fraction of the second margin *minus* the first.

[4] In so far as short-period fluctuations affect the amount of cash obtainable on the security of the bonds they will tend to raise the value of β.

2. We may still say something more about the value of γ. If the present price of Consols is p and the holder has a certain more or less definite idea based on past experience about the minimum to which this price may fall, p_{min}, it is plausible to assume that γ is proportionate to $\dfrac{p - p_{min}}{p}$, i.e. to the maximum percentage by which the price of Consols is considered apt to fall. We thus have

$$\gamma = g\frac{p - p_{min}}{p} = g\left(1 - \frac{p_{min}}{p}\right). \qquad . \qquad . \quad (3)$$

If the period for which the calculation is made is one year and the depreciation was considered certain, g would be equal to 100. But since the period is normally longer and the maximum depreciation not very probable, g may be expected to be rather small as compared with one hundred.

As the price of Consols is in inverse proportion to their yield, the expression (3) may be written

$$\gamma = g\left(1 - \frac{r}{r_{max}}\right) \qquad . \qquad . \qquad . \quad (3a)$$

where r_{max} is the yield corresponding to the "minimum price" p_{min}. By substituting this expression for γ in the equation (2) we obtain, after simple transformations,

$$r = \frac{\rho_e}{1 + \dfrac{g}{r_{max}}} + \frac{\beta + g}{1 + \dfrac{g}{r_{max}}}. \qquad . \qquad . \quad (4)$$

If the coefficients β, g, and r_{max} are stable, this equation expresses the long-term rate r as a linear function of the expected short-term rate ρ_e. It is easy to see that (g, β, and r_{max} being stable) r always changes by a smaller amount than ρ_e, since $1 + \dfrac{g}{r_{max}} > 1$. This is the result of our assumption that as r increases the risk of the depreciation of Consols declines (equation $3a$).

We have thus *two* factors explaining the stability of the long-term rate as compared with the short-term rate of interest.

(1) The short-period changes of the short-term rate ρ are only partly reflected in the estimates of ρ_e. (2) The long-term rate r changes by a smaller amount than the average short-term rate ρ_e expected over the next few years.

3. It is important to notice that the " risk coefficient " (which is a marginal concept) may increase not only when the depreciation of bonds is considered more likely but also when the proportion of long-term assets held to short-term assets + cash rises. For then with the same probability of bond depreciation the latter, if it happens, means a greater loss relative to the value of all liquid assets. This " increasing risk " is accounted for by a higher g. Thus if, *ceteris paribus*, the amount of long-term assets relative to all liquid assets held by the public rises, g tends to increase. Moreover, if income tax—from which we have so far abstracted—is in existence, g is not a pure risk coefficient, but depends on the rates of income tax as well. Indeed, the difference between the long-term rate and the short-term rate is subject to tax, but the depreciation in bonds is not allowed for in tax assessment.[1] Thus if g were the pure risk coefficient $\gamma = g\left(1 - \dfrac{r}{r_{max}}\right)$ would cover only the difference $r - \rho_e$ after taxation. To cover the *actual* difference $r - \rho_e$, the coefficient g must be correspondingly higher.[2] If, for instance, the tax is 5s. in the £ and there is no surtax, $g = \dfrac{4}{3}$ of the pure risk coefficient. If surtax exists it is not possible to establish such a simple relation because the tax incidence is then not even.

Application to the Yields of Consols, 1849-1938

1. We shall now apply the results arrived at in the last section to the analysis of yields of Consols in the period 1849-1938.

---

[1] This is true of the U.K.; in the U.S.A., however, a part of the loss from sales of bonds *is* allowed for in income tax assessment and therefore our subsequent argument does not apply strictly to that country.

[2] This problem does not arise with regard to β because this represents a loss in income which is allowed for in taxation.

Their time curve is given in Figure 4.   It may be seen that it is possible to subdivide this period into ten very unequal intervals, in each of which the long-term rate undergoes relatively small fluctuations round the average as compared with the changes between the intervals : 1849-80 ; 1881-87, 1888-93, 1894-1900, 1901-09, 1910-14, 1915-18, 1919-21, 1922-31, 1932-38.   This may be accounted for by an hypothesis that within each of these intervals the expected short-term rate ρ_e and the coefficients g, $r_{\max}$, and β fluctuated rather slightly around certain values while

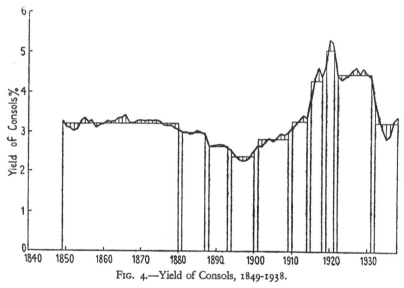

Fig. 4.—Yield of Consols, 1849-1938.

they underwent long-run changes from interval to interval.   Let us turn our attention to such changes of the expected average discount rate ρ_e.   Within each of our intervals the discount rate ρ underwent in fact strong fluctuations which did not, however, cause important fluctuations of ρ_e.   This may be accounted for by the following hypothesis : the investors disregarded to a great extent in their estimates of ρ_e the " high " and " low " levels of the discount rate within the intervals, classifying them as temporary, and based their expectations chiefly on the last " medium " position ; and the spread of these " medium values " was rather small within each period. If this hypothesis is correct, it follows that the average ρ_e in each period does not differ much from the average of the actual rate of discount ρ in that period. This is very important for our inquiry. For on this assumption we may take the average discount rate in each period to be the first approximation of the average ρ_e. Thus we may correlate the average yields of Consols and average discount rates in our periods and analyse the regression equations by means of our formula (4).

2. The data are given in Table VI :

TABLE VI

Yield of Consols and Discount Rate

Interval.	Average Yield of Consols (%).	Average Discount Rate (%).
1849-80	3·21	3·66
1881-87	2·98	2·82
1888-93	2·63	2·68
1894-1900	2·38	2·18
1901-09	2·82	3·09
1910-14	3·27	3·4
1915-18	4·30	4·3
1919-21	5·07	5·09
1922-31	4·48	3·76
1932-38	3·25	0·82

We now plot these figures on a scatter diagram (Fig. 5). It will be seen that most of the points lie very close to two straight lines AB and A_1B_1. The points corresponding to the intervals before the last war lie close to AB except those corresponding to 1881-87 and 1910-14. The points corresponding to the post-war periods lie close to the line A_1B_1, which is considerably above AB. Finally, the war period 1915-18 is represented by a point lying between AB and A_1B_1. It must be noticed at once that the position of the point 1881-87 above AB is fully accounted for by the fact that the yield of Consols in this period did not reflect the level of the " pure long-term rate," being " too high " because of the expected conversion.[1]

The results obtained may be plausibly interpreted in terms of our formula (4). In the period 1849-1909 the coefficients g, r_{max}, and β were more or less stable, and therefore we have a linear functional relation between r and ρ_e, represented by AB. After this period these coefficients underwent a strong change,

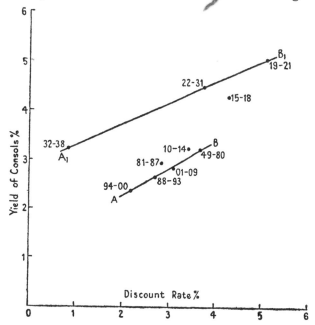

Fig. 5.—Discount Rate and Yield of Consols, 1849-1938.

chiefly during the last war, and then became stable again in the post-war period, so that the points ρ_e, r are in this period again situated on the straight line A_1B_1. The points 1910-14 and 1915-18 lying between AB and A_1B_1 represent the period during which the shift from AB to A_1B_1 occurred.

3. From the equations of the lines AB and A_1B_1 the coefficients g and β may be now obtained for the pre-war and post-war period respectively.

[1] See R. G. Hawtrey, *A Century of Bank Rate.*

The equation of AB (pre-war period) is

$$r = 0.550\rho_e + 1.17.$$

If we compare it with our formula (3),

$$r = \frac{\rho_e}{1 + \frac{g}{r_{max}}} + \frac{\beta + g}{1 + \frac{g}{r_{max}}},$$

we obtain two equations

$$\frac{1}{1 + \frac{g}{r_{max}}} = 0.550 \quad \text{and} \quad \frac{\beta + g}{1 + \frac{g}{r_{max}}} = 1.17.$$

Now as to the expected maximum long-term rate we may assume that it is approximately 3.4, for this was the maximum rate in the period in question and the level of r at the beginning of it was not much lower. It is then possible to obtain from the last equations the coefficients g and β. We have $g = 2.78$, $\beta = -0.65$.

The equation for the post-war period is

$$r = 0.425\rho_e + 2.90,$$

and consequently

$$\frac{1}{1 + \frac{g}{r_{max}}} = 0.425 \quad \text{and} \quad \frac{\beta + g}{1 + \frac{g}{r_{max}}} = 2.90.$$

Here r_{max} may be assumed equal to 5.1, this being the level reached at the beginning of the period and never exceeded afterwards. Thus we obtain $g = 6.9$, $\beta = -0.07$.[1]

We may now put together the results of our calculation:

Period.	g.	r_{max}.	β.
1849-1909	2.78	3.40	— 0.65
1919-38	6.90	5.10	— 0.07

[1] It is perhaps more correct to assume that in the interval 1932-38 r_{max} was lower than 5.1, say 4.5. We then obtain for this interval $g = 6.03$, $\beta = 0.73$. The positive value for β in this interval is quite plausible in view of the unusually low margin between the discount rate and the rate on loans to the discount market (cf. p. 38).

From the point of view of the confirmation of our theory the most important result is that β (the balance of disadvantages and advantages of bonds as compared with bills apart from the risk of depreciation) is small, as we expected it to be for theoretical reasons.   If the coefficient of ρ_e in the post-war period had been not 0·425 but, say, 0·25, we should, *ceteris paribus*, have obtained for β the value — 3·7, which would be obviously absurd and so disprove our theory.

The coefficient g is—again in accordance with *a priori* argument—small as compared with 100, both in the pre-war and the post-war periods.   (The " pure " risk coefficient is even smaller because g is inflated by income tax, cf. p. 40.)   The tremendous rise in g (about 2·5 times) between these two periods is explained by the much stronger fluctuations in r after 1914 and by the rise in income tax and surtax.   The strong rise in g in combination with the increase in r_{max} accounts for the shift of the line AB to the position A_1B_1.

4. It is interesting to notice that during this war the movement of the long-term rate conforms to the 1919-38 formula. The average discount rate ρ was 1·04 per cent in 1940 and 1·03 per cent in 1941.   This was probably also the level expected for the next few years.   Substituting these values into the 1919-38 formula,

$$r = 0·425\rho_e + 2·90,$$

we obtain about 3·34 per cent for both years.   The actual average yields of Consols were : 3·40 per cent in 1940 and 3·13 per cent in 1941.   The agreement between the calculated and the actual values is thus very close.   This is the more surprising in that the increase in income tax tended to increase g.

It is necessary to take into account here that g depends *inter alia* on the ratio of long-term assets held to short-term assets + cash (see p. 40) and thus the Government borrowing policy determines within certain limits the long-term rate of interest.   If the Government borrows a part of the amounts required on long-term at a certain fixed rate and the rest on short-term—as it was in fact the case during this war—the long-term rate is actually fixed by the Government. This is, however, only the case if this rate is chosen so that the Government is able to sell *some* amount of its long-term issues. If the Government long-term rate of borrowing is so low that nobody is prepared to lend at this rate, the Government must finance all the Budget deficit by floating debt. It loses then the control of the long-term rate unless it is prepared to borrow short over and above the deficit requirements and buy long-term securities from the public.

3. A THEORY OF PROFITS

The Determinants of Profits

1. In this essay we attempt to investigate the determinants of profits in short and long periods. The short-period analysis will consist in relating the profits in a given short period to certain factors operating in the preceding periods. From this we shall pass to the examination of the level of the rate of profit in long periods, in particular in relation to the rate of interest.

We abstract in our argument from the influence on profits of the balance of foreign trade and the Budget deficit (or surplus). We therefore assume a closed system and a balanced State Budget. It is, consequently, quite clear that our conclusions are by no means applicable to a war economy. Our aim is, on the contrary, to examine the problem of profits in a closed *laissez-faire* system. In concert with abstracting from the Budget deficit we also assume that no interest on the National Debt is paid.

By gross profits we shall mean depreciation and maintenance, net undistributed profits, dividends, interest, rent and also managerial salaries, all *after payment of direct taxes*.[1] The receivers of this type of income we call capitalists. The rest of incomes (also taken net of direct taxes) are wages, small salaries (for the sake of brevity we shall use below " salaries " for small salaries), and doles. The saving out of these incomes is assumed to be small as compared with total saving, and is neglected for the sake of simplicity—i.e. equated to nought.

2. We shall now establish the fundamental equation between profits on the one hand and capitalists' consumption and private investment on the other. We must, however, first define certain concepts. By gross investment we shall mean the value of all sales of newly produced fixed capital equipment + increase in working capital and stocks ; and by gross national income the

---

[1] However, taxes accruing but not yet paid—i.e. increase in tax reserves *are* included in profits.

sum of total personal consumption and gross investment. We shall distinguish private and Government investment (armaments, Government buildings, etc.). The gross national income so defined is, as may easily be seen, also equal to profits gross of depreciation and net of direct taxes + wages, salaries and doles (also net of taxes) + Government investment. For the proceeds of sales of consumption and investment goods [1] will be received by capitalists and workers employed by them, or passed by means of indirect and direct taxes to the Government, which will, in turn, spend the revenue either on wages and salaries of Government employees and doles or Government investment. We thus have the following " balance sheet " of national income and expenditure :

Gross profits (gross of depreciation but net of direct taxes)	Total gross investment
	Capitalists' consumption
Wages, salaries and doles (net of direct taxes)	Workers' consumption
Gross Government investment	
Gross national income	Gross national income.

Now, since wages, salaries and doles are, as assumed above, fully spent on consumption, and total gross investment − gross Government investment = gross private investment, it follows directly that

$$\text{Gross profits} = \text{Gross private investment} + \text{Capitalists' consumption.} \qquad (1)$$

What is the proper meaning of this equation ? Does it mean that profits in a certain period determine capitalists' consumption and investment, or the other way round ? The answer to this question depends on which of these items is directly subject to the decisions of capitalists. Now, it is clear that they may decide to consume and to invest more in a certain short period than in the preceding period, but they cannot decide to earn

[1] The latter inclusive of the increase in working capital and stocks. When this type of investment does not actually involve a sale, it may be considered as a firm's sale to itself.

more. It is therefore their investment and consumption decisions which determine profits, and not vice versa.

If the period which we consider is short, we may say that capitalists' investment and consumption are determined by decisions formed in the *past*. For the execution of investment orders takes a certain time, and as to the capitalists' consumption, it is only with a certain delay that the capitalists' standard of living reacts to the change of factors which influence it.

If capitalists decided always to consume and to invest in a given period what they have earned in the preceding period, the profits in the given period would be equal to those in the preceding one. In such case they would remain stationary, and the problem of how to read the above equation would lose its importance. But such is *not* the case. Although profits in the preceding periods are one of the important determinants of capitalists' consumption and investment, capitalists in general do *not* decide to consume and invest in a given month what they have earned in the preceding one. This explains why profits are *not* stationary, but fluctuate in time.

3. The above argument requires a certain qualification. The past investment decisions may not fully determine the volume of investment in a given period, owing to unexpected accumulation or running down of stocks. The importance of this factor seems, however, to have been frequently exaggerated.

A second qualification arises out of the fact that these decisions will usually be in real terms, and in the meantime prices may change. For instance, a piece of ordered capital equipment may cost more than at the period when the order was given. To get over this difficulty it will be convenient to deflate both sides of the equation by appropriate price indices. We thus obtain an equation between real gross profits and real capitalists' consumption + real gross private investment.

We may now conclude that the real gross profits in a given short period are determined by decisions of capitalists as to their consumption and investment formed in the past, subject to the correction for unexpected changes in the volume of stocks.

There arises here the problem what will be the place of the factors determining the distribution of the national income in this theory. Since profits in a given short period are determined by capitalists' decisions as to their consumption and investment formed in the past, the factors determining the distribution of income will affect not real profits but the real wage and salary bill—and consequently the national output. If, for instance, the degree of market imperfection or oligopoly increases, and, as a result, so does the ratio of profits to wages, real profits do not change, but the real wage bill falls, first, because of the fall in real wage rates, and secondly, because of the consequent reduction in demand for wage goods, and thus of output and employment in the wage-good industries. (If salary rates do not rise relative to wage rates the real salary bill falls as well.) Percentage gross margins increase, but the national output falls just so much that, as a result, the real total profits remain the same. However great the margin of profit on a unit of output, the capitalists cannot make more in total profits than they consume and invest (inclusive of accumulation of unsold goods).[1]

4. The above analysis obviously cannot answer the question why the rate of profit taken as an average for longer periods is higher than the rate of interest. It only relates profits in a given short period to capitalists' consumption and investment in this period determined by factors which operated in the preceding periods. To say something about the actual level of profits it is necessary to apply a different type of analysis.

The Rate of Profit in the Long Period

1. The long-run analysis is often conducted under the assumption of long-run equilibrium *sensu stricto* (i.e. in the sense that the system is at rest). This is entirely unjustified, because we *know* that apart from cyclical fluctuations the economic system is subject to a complex process of long-run development. We shall

[1] The theory of profits presented here is closely allied to Lord Keynes' theory of saving and investment. It has been, however, developed independently of Lord Keynes in my " Essai d'une théorie du mouvement cyclique des affaires," *Revue d'économie politique*, Mars-Avril 1935, and " A Macrodynamic Theory of Business Cycles," *Econometrica*, July 1935.

therefore approach the problem from a different angle : we shall simply consider connections between averages of variables in a period extending over a full business cycle and chosen so that its beginning and end are positions half-way between boom and slump.

We shall assume that the average change of any variable per year of our period is small as compared with the average of this variable over this period. That means that if the period considered consists of years 1, 2, 3, . . . n, and is preceded by a year 0, we assume for any variable X that $\dfrac{X_n - X_0}{n}$ is small as compared with $\dfrac{X_1 + X_2 + X_3 + \ldots + X_n}{n}$. This condition is likely to be fulfilled in reality, since our period covers a full cycle and the economic development after elimination of the trade cycle is usually " slow."

The assumption of the " slowness " of long-run economic development is of great significance for the long-period analysis. Indeed, when short periods are considered, any relation between two variables involves time lags. For instance, investment at a given moment is a function of factors which operated some time ago. Now, if these time-lags are short—say, not greater than of an order of a year—they may be disregarded in our long-period analysis. For, since $\dfrac{X_n - X_0}{n}$ is small as compared with $\dfrac{X_1 + X_2 + \ldots + X_n}{n}$, the latter differs little from $\dfrac{X_0 + X_1 + \ldots + X_{n-1}}{n}$; thus, when the influence of X upon the situation in a given long period is examined, we shall make only a small error by taking into consideration the former instead of the latter.

2. In every year of our period gross profit is equal to capitalists' consumption + private gross investment. (For the sake of brevity we shall use below " investment " for private investment.) Thus the average gross profit is equal to the average capitalists' consumption + average gross investment. If we deduct from

both sides of this equation the average depreciation and maintenance, we find that the average net profit $\overline{P}$ is equal to the average capitalists' consumption $\overline{C}$ + the average net investment $\overline{I}$,

$$\overline{P} = \overline{C} + \overline{I} \quad . \qquad . \qquad . \qquad . \quad (2)$$

where $\overline{C}$ and $\overline{I}$ are understood here to be expressed in real terms —namely, calculated at prices prevailing at the beginning of the period considered, and also $\overline{P}$ is the average " real " profit.

We may make the following assumption, plausible as a first approximation, about the " real " capitalists' consumption C_t in a given year: that it consists of a stable part A and a part proportionate to the real profit $P_{t-\psi}$ of some time ago : [1]

$$C_t = A + \lambda P_{t-\psi}. \qquad . \qquad . \qquad . \quad (3)$$

ψ indicates thus the delay of the reaction of capitalists' consumption to the change in their current income ; it is probably of an order of a year or less. λ is positive and < 1.[2] Finally, A is the result of habits acquired by capitalists as a result of past long-run development. It changes, therefore, slowly in time, also in the period considered, but the time lags involved are very long, and therefore we shall assume A in the period considered (which, covering a full cycle, is about 10 years long) to be determined by factors which operated prior to it. We take now the average of both sides of our equation (3) over our period. Since the time-lag ψ is relatively short, it may be neglected according to the argument of the preceding section. We thus obtain

$$\overline{C} = \overline{A} + \lambda\overline{P}, . \qquad . \qquad . \qquad . \quad (4)$$

and from this equation and equation (2) it follows

$$\overline{P} = \frac{\overline{A} + \overline{I}}{1 - \lambda} \qquad . \qquad . \qquad . \qquad . \quad (5)$$

---

[1] We neglect the influence of the rate of interest upon capitalists' consumption as not very important.

[2] A tentative estimate of λ for the U.S.A. in the period 1925-35 suggests that it was < 0.33. (Undistributed profits were, of course, included in capitalists' incomes.)

where $\bar{A}$ depends on the development preceding the period considered.[1]

3. In order to obtain a formula for the average *rate* of profit in our period, we shall now consider the average volume of total capital in this period. Let K_0 be the value of total capital equipment at current prices of investment goods at the beginning of this period. Since $\bar{I}$ is the average net " real " investment in our period at prices prevailing at the beginning of our period, the " real " capital at the end of the period is $K_0 + n\bar{I}$, where n is length of the period.

Now, the deviations of the annual rate of investment from the average annual rate of investment $\bar{I}$ throughout the period may be assumed small (say, of the order of 2 or 3 per cent) as compared with the initial volume of capital equipment K_0. It may be shown that if this is the case then with $n = 10$ years, say, the average volume of capital $\bar{K}$ will differ little from the average of its volume at the beginning and at the end of the period. We have thus as a good approximation

$$\bar{K} = K_0 + \frac{n}{2}\bar{I}. \qquad . \qquad . \qquad . \qquad (6)$$

4. We shall now obtain a formula for the average rate of profit in our period which we may determine as the ratio of average *money* profit to average *money* value of capital at current prices. Thus, before dividing $\bar{P}$ by $\bar{K}$, which are " real " values calculated at prices at the beginning of the period, they should be multiplied by appropriate price indices. It is, however, easy to see that this correction will be important only if the average of the price index of consumption goods related to the beginning of the period as basis differs considerably from that of investment

---

[1] It must be noticed that equation (3), and consequently equations (4) and (5), cease to be plausible in the case where taxation is heavy, and its system is such that the tax on profits increases much quicker than profits (for instance, Excess Profits Tax). For although profits $P_{t-\psi}$ are net of taxes paid, they include taxes accruing but not yet paid—i.e. the increase in tax reserves ; and if this part of profits is considerable it may affect capitalists' consumption decisions. Now, as long as the tax is on a proportionate basis, our formula, it may be shown, still holds good approximately, although λ and ψ will have then a more complex meaning. However, if taxation is strongly disproportionate, the formula becomes invalid.

goods. Since, however, the beginning of the period has been chosen in such a way that it represents a half-way position between boom and slump, this is unlikely to be the case, and therefore $\overline{P}/\overline{K}$ may be taken as a first approximation to the average rate of profit π in our period. We thus obtain

$$\pi = \frac{1}{1 - \lambda} \frac{\overline{A} + \overline{I}}{K_0 + \frac{n}{2}\overline{I}}. \qquad . \qquad . \qquad . \quad (7)$$

If we denote $\overline{A}/K_0$ by α, and $\overline{I}/K_0$ by i, we have after simple transformations

$$\pi = \frac{2}{n(1 - \lambda)} \frac{\alpha + i}{\frac{2}{n} + i}. \qquad . \qquad . \quad (7a)$$

Since both $\overline{A}$ (the average of the stable part of capitalists' consumption) and K_0 (the value of capital at the beginning of the period) are fully determined by development prior to this period, $\alpha = \dfrac{\overline{A}}{K_0}$ may be considered given. Thus the average rate of profit π is represented as a function of i—i.e. of the ratio of average investment $\overline{I}$ to the initial value of capital K_0.[1]

As will be seen in the last essay, $\overline{I}$ depends on a variety of factors. We shall try to arrive here at certain results from the discussion of the formula (7a) without going into the problems of the determination of i.

The Rate of Profit and the Rate of Interest in the Long Period

The problem which concerns us here is what causes the rate of profit to be higher than the rate of interest in the long period and whether this must be the case under all circumstances.[2]

---

[1] It may seem from equation (7) that π falls when the length of the full cycle n increases. But it must not be forgotten that, since A, the stable part of capitalists' consumption, changes within this period, its average $\overline{A}$ depends on its length. Therefore π may not be affected by the change in n.

[2] As profits are understood throughout the argument to be after taxation, the rate of interest, when compared with the rate of profit as given by formula (7a), must also be taken after deduction of income tax.

1. It may be seen directly from the formula ($7a$) that if $\alpha \geqslant \dfrac{2}{n}$ the average rate of profit $\pi \geqslant \dfrac{2}{n(1 - \lambda)}$. Since n is about 10 years, it follows at once that the rate of profit is greater than 20 per cent.

In this case the fact that the rate of profit is higher than the rate of interest would be very simply explained. The rate of profit, whatever the rate of investment, is above a certain level. The rate of interest determined by the volume of transactions and supply of cash by banks [1] is below this limit. The latter is subject to the qualification that no " over full employment " is then involved ; for in such a state the increasing volume of transactions and thus increasing demand for cash may drive the rate of interest to a very high level. It is unlikely, however, that it should reach the level of the rate of profit because this would imply a very low rate of investment and thus most probably a low level of employment.

We shall now consider the case of $\alpha < \dfrac{2}{n}$ which is of much greater practical importance.

2. In this case the average rate of profit $\pi < \dfrac{2}{n(1 - \lambda)}.$ It is also easy to see from formula ($7a$) that π is an increasing function of i. For if i increases by a certain amount, the numerator of the fraction $\dfrac{\alpha + i}{\dfrac{2}{n} + i}$ increases if $\alpha < \dfrac{2}{n}$ in a higher proportion than the denominator.

It follows directly that to obtain the lower limit of the rate of profit we must substitute into the formula ($7a$) the lowest level to which i may fall. Now, i is the ratio of the average net investment in our period to the value of capital at its beginning. If investment activity is at a complete standstill $i = - d$, where

---

[1] These factors determine directly the *short-term* rate of interest (see p. 36). The *long-term* rate of interest is determined by the expected short-term rate and by certain risk factors and income tax (see pp. 39 and 40). It should be remembered that it is the interest *net* of tax which is relevant for our argument.

d is depreciation and maintenance in per cent of capital. But because some repairs are always carried out, $i_{min} > -d$.[1] We thus obtain the lowest limit for the rate of profit,

$$\pi \geqslant \pi_{min} = \frac{2}{n(1-\lambda)} \frac{\alpha + i_{min}}{\dfrac{2}{n} + i_{min}}. \qquad . \qquad . \quad (8)$$

Let us assume now for the moment that the short-term rate of interest, and in consequence also the long-term rate of interest, is kept by banking policy at a certain definite level r. The condition for the rate of profit being always higher than the rate of interest is then

$$\frac{2}{n(1-\lambda)} \frac{\alpha + i_{min}}{\dfrac{2}{n} + i_{min}} > r. \qquad . \qquad . \quad (9)$$

From this inequality may be obtained the level above which α must be in order that the rate of profit shall always be higher than the rate of interest. If, for instance, $\lambda = 0.3$, $n = 10$, $i_{min} = -0.04$ and $r = 0.04$, we obtain from (9) $\alpha > 5.0$ per cent. Thus if α is higher than 5.0 per cent, the average rate of profit is always higher than the long-term rate of interest, which is kept at the level of 4 per cent.

3. It follows from the argument in the last two paragraphs that if α is above the " critical level " the rate of profit is *always* higher than the rate of interest.

On the other hand, if α is at the " critical level " (which makes the expression on the left-hand side equal to the rate of interest) the rate of profit may fall to the level of the rate of interest if $i = i_{min}$. There arise here two problems : (1) Is it possible that investment activity may remain in our long period at the minimum level so that i is actually equal to i_{min} ? (2) If this happened in one of our periods, and thus the average rate of

---

[1] As capital consists not only of fixed capital but of working capital and stocks as well i_{min} may be lower than $-d$ if inventories are being run down at more than d per cent per annum.

profit was equal to the rate of interest in that period, can this position persist in the next long period?

Let us consider the first question. If investment activity is maintained throughout the period at its minimum level the average rate of profit is equal to the rate of interest. Investment I being stable (at the minimum level throughout the period) the rate of profit undergoes only small changes within the period because both the stable part of capitalists' consumption and the volume of fixed capital K change slowly. Therefore the rate of profit does not differ much throughout the period from the average and thus is close to the rate of interest. But if the rate of profit is close to the rate of interest throughout the period, investment activity is likely to be maintained at the minimum level because no margin to cover rent on land, management costs, and risk is provided. Thus $i = i_{min}$ *is* a possible state of affairs.[1]

Let us now consider the second problem. Imagine that α is at the " critical level " and in one of our long periods $i = i_{min}$; the average rate of profit in that period is consequently equal to the rate of interest. Do developments in this period prepare the ground for a higher rate of profit in the next full-cycle period? Certainly i, which $= i_{min}$ in the period considered, is negative, therefore the capital K_0 at the beginning of the next period will be smaller. And this will tend to increase α of the next period, which is the ratio of the average of the stable part of capitalists' consumption $\bar{A}$ to the capital K_0 at the beginning of the period. However, dis-saving, which takes place in the period considered, will certainly tend to depress the stable part of capitalists' consumption in the next period: the less wealthy the capitalists feel the less is the amount they are apt to consume irrespective of their current income. Also the persistence of a very low capitalists' income in the period considered will tend to press down the capitalists' customary standard of living, and this will be reflected in the fall in the stable part of their consumption A in the next period.

Thus not only will K_0 at the beginning of the next period be smaller, but so also is likely to be $\bar{A}$ in that period. It is thus

[1] In this case there are actually no cyclical fluctuations, cf. p. 75, below.

not at all certain that $\alpha = \dfrac{\overline{A}}{K_0}$ will increase. And if it remains at the same level as in the period considered, nothing has happened to push upwards the rate of profit, which may thus continue to be equal to the rate of interest.

If α falls *below* the " critical level " the rate of profit will be below the rate of interest when investment activity is at the minimum level. It may be demonstrated in the same way as above that this state of affairs is possible and may persist over a number of long periods.

4. So far we have assumed that the rate of interest is given. If, however, investment activity falls—as was assumed in the last section—to its minimum level, total output and employment must shrink considerably ; the demand for cash for transactions is greatly reduced, and, as a result, the short-term rate of interest tends to fall, and is followed by the long-term rate. However, the short-term rate cannot fall below zero, and the long-term rate, because of the risk involved in the fluctuations of the price of bonds, below a positive value r_{min}. Thus, if α is sufficiently low, the fall of the rate of interest cannot prevent the possibility of the rate of profit reaching the level of the rate of interest. Indeed, there is always such a value of α at which the lower limit of the rate of profit π_{min} is equal to the lower limit of the rate of interest r_{min}.

5. In the light of the above argument, the relation between the rate of profit and the rate of interest in long periods depends to a great extent on the value of α (the ratio of the average of the stable part of capitalists' consumption over the period $\overline{A}$ to the volume of capital K_0 at the beginning of the period). If α is above the " critical level " (which depends on the rate of interest) the rate of profit is *always* higher than the rate of interest. If α is at the " critical level " (or below it), and investment activity is at its minimum level, the rate of profit is equal to the rate of interest (or falls short of it). Such a state of " long-period deadlock " is by no means excluded and may even last for a number of long periods.

Part Two

BUSINESS CYCLE AND TREND

4. THE "PURE" BUSINESS CYCLE

THE theory of the business cycle presented below is in many respects similar to that given in my *Essays in the Theory of Economic Fluctuations* and my earlier writings. The justification for this new version is that: (1) I now tackle the problem from a new angle and introduce new factors into the explanation of the business cycle; (2) with this new treatment it is possible to drop some of my simplifying assumptions and to achieve some new results; (3) I do not now consider only the problem of the "pure" business cycle, but deal in the last essay with the trend superimposed on the cycle.

Investment and Profits

1. We make the same assumptions as in the preceding essay, i.e. we consider a closed economic system with a balanced State Budget and abstract from working class savings. We thus have the equation

$$P = C + I \quad . \qquad . \qquad . \qquad . \quad (1)$$

where P are net real profits, C real capitalists' consumption, and I real net investment. If we denote by R the real depreciation and maintenance (i.e. replacement required to maintain capital intact, which we shall call "required replacement"), $I + R$ is the real gross investment. As in the preceding essay we assume the following interrelation between capitalist consumption C and profits P (see p. 52):

$$C_t = A_t + \lambda P_{t-\varphi}. \qquad . \qquad . \quad (2)$$

A_t, the stable part of capitalists' consumption, is the result of habits acquired by capitalists in the past long-run development.

(A_t changes slowly in time but is not subject to cyclical fluctuations. We shall consequently assume it constant for the discussion of the " pure " business cycle and reintroduce this factor only in the next essay where the trend problem will be considered.) λ, which is the capitalists' marginal propensity to consume, is positive and substantially less than 1. Finally, ψ indicates the delay of the reaction of the capitalists' consumption to the change in their current income.

2. From the equations (1) and (2) it follows

$$P_t - \lambda P_{t-\psi} = A_t + I_t. \qquad . \qquad . \qquad (3)$$

Now it may be shown that if the change of P_t can be assumed approximately linear in a period of a length of the order of ψ, we may write

$$P_t - \lambda P_{t-\psi} = (1 - \lambda)P_{t+\kappa} \qquad . \qquad . \qquad (4)$$

where κ is determined by the formula $\kappa = \dfrac{\lambda}{1 - \lambda}\psi.$[1]

It follows directly from equations (3) and (4)

$$P_{t+\kappa} = \frac{A_t + I_t}{1 - \lambda},$$

or, which amounts to the same,

$$P_t = \frac{A_{t-\kappa} + I_{t-\kappa}}{1 - \lambda}. \qquad . \qquad . \qquad (5)$$

This is nothing else than the " multiplier equation " for profits in which there is involved a time-lag κ. The "multiplier" $= \dfrac{1}{1 - \lambda}.$

---

[1] Equation (4) is equivalent to

$$P_t = \lambda P_{t-\psi} + (1 - \lambda)P_{t+\kappa}.$$

Under the above assumptions κ fulfils approximately the condition

$$\lambda(t - \psi) + (1 - \lambda)(t + \kappa) = t,$$

from which follows $\kappa = \dfrac{\lambda}{1 - \lambda}\psi.$ If ψ is shorter than a year and λ smaller than 1/3 (cf. footnote to p. 52), κ is shorter than half a year.

The Determinants of the Rate of Investment Decisions

1. We are now going to discuss the much more intricate problem of the determinants of the rate of investment decisions. Let us consider a short period dt. The investment plans undertaken before this period have been pushed up to a point where they cease to be profitable owing to the imperfection of the market for products on the one hand and to the imperfection of the capital market and " increasing risk " [1] on the other. What happens then in the period dt to cause new investment plans to emerge?

There may, of course, occur a rise in the prospective rate of profit (or a fall in the rate of interest) owing to the change in the economic situation in dt, and this would cause an expansion of the investment plans at the end of this period as compared with its beginning. We shall consider this reason for new investment later on in some detail. But provided that such a change has not occurred, will new investment decisions—taking the objective form of investment orders—not be forthcoming at all in the period dt? What is the factor which may cause new investment decisions in the absence of a change of the prospective rate of profit (or the rate of interest)? This factor is the inflow of new gross savings (i.e. of net saving + depreciation and maintenance) which will push forward the barriers set to investment plans by the limited accessibility of the capital market and " increasing risk."

2. Before we proceed to a detailed consideration of this influence it should be remembered that real gross savings in any period of time are equal to the real gross investment, i.e. required replacement R + real net investment I. Thus in the period dt real gross savings $= (R + I)dt$. (The rate of real gross investment $R + I$ in the period dt must not, of course, be confused with the rate of investment *decisions* in that period; the actual investment in dt is the result of *past* investment decisions.)

---

[1] See my *Essays in the Theory of Economic Fluctuations*, " The Principle of Increasing Risk," pp. 95-106. According to this principle the larger the investment in fixed equipment undertaken by an entrepreneur with given own capital, the greater its marginal risk. See also J. Steindl, " On Risk," *Oxford Economic Papers*, No. 5.

A part of the new savings $(R + I)dt$ accrues to " entrepreneurs," i.e. to enterprises directly (undistributed profits) or to people ready to absorb the new issues of shares of enterprises. The rest of savings accumulates in the hands of " pure rentiers " holding their savings exclusively in deposits or bonds.[1] If we denote the real " rentiers " savings by s, the gross real savings of the entrepreneurs are $R + (I - s)$. Let us first consider a special case when $I - s = 0$. The gross saving of entrepreneurs in the period dt is then equal to the required replacement Rdt, and if they reinvest this amount in fixed capital they do not strike against the barriers of the limited accessibility of the capital market or " increasing risk " because they do not increase their commitments. Thus the rate of investment decisions is here R. We shall now consider the general case where $I - s$ is not equal to zero.

Prima facie it looks as if what was said about reinvestment of R remains true of $R + (I - s)$. For the entrepreneurs as a body when deciding to invest anew $[R + (I - s)]dt$ will not increase their indebtedness at the end of the period as compared with the level at its beginning. Two factors must, however, be taken into consideration. First, what is relevant is not absolute but relative commitments. If the ratio of the fixed entrepreneurs' capital to their own capital is δ they can invest $[R + \delta(I - s)]dt$ (where $\delta > 1$) without increasing their *degree* of commitment. Secondly, a decision to invest not only Rdt but also $\delta(I - s)dt$ means (when $I - s$ is positive) a decision to expand equipment. Now if the objective factors determining the profitability of investment are unchanged and the investment is in the line of entrepreneur's production, this means, because of market imperfection for his products, a smaller prospective rate of profit although the economic situation has not changed. And shifting to new fields means a higher risk. Thus new investment decisions may be represented by a formula $[R + \eta\delta(I - s)]dt$ where $\eta < 1$ and $\delta > 1$. The same formula will hold good for the case when $I - s$ is negative.

---

[1] In fact there does not exist such a sharp line of division : what we consider here is rather a simplified model being a first approximation to the real world.

Since $\eta < 1$ and $\delta > 1$ it is uncertain whether $\eta\delta$ is higher or lower than 1. We shall make a plausible assumption that the degree of indebtedness of " entrepreneurs " towards " rentiers " is not very high and thus δ only moderately exceeds 1 ; and on the other hand that the limitation in reinvestment imposed on " entrepreneurs " savings by market imperfection and the high risk of investment in alien fields make for a rather low η. In these conditions $\eta\delta$ is likely to be lower than 1 and this will be assumed throughout the argument. We shall denote $\eta\delta$ by $1 - c$ where c is positive and < 1.

3. We have assumed so far that in the period dt there was no change in the economic situation which would influence the prospective rate of profit (or the rate of interest). We shall now consider this problem. The two most important determinants of the prospective rate of profit may be considered to be the real profits P and the volume of capital equipment. The larger P and the smaller the existing capital equipment the larger will be in general the prospective rates of profit on new investment.[1] The influence of the prices of new investment goods upon the prospective rates of profit is roughly accounted for by taking into consideration the *real* profits P. This allowance for changes in the prices of investment goods may prove insufficient for two reasons : (1) the prices of investment goods may not change in the same proportion as the prices which are used to deflate profits ; (2) what is more important, the entrepreneur takes into account in his investment decisions not only the current situation but also the uncertain future ; the present money profits cannot be expected to last over all the life of the investment, but only in the near future ; but the price he pays for investment goods is a determinant of the prospective rate of profit which is fixed once and for all. Therefore the rise in prices of investment goods usually accompanying the rise in real profits will weaken the effect of the latter upon investment decisions.

If the real profits P increase in the period dt by dP we can say, according to the above, that this will push the investment plans by adP. a is here by no means a constant, but a positive

---

[1] Cf. my *Essays*, pp. 132-140.

co-efficient susceptible to various types of changes and reflecting, *inter alia*, the influence of changes in the prices of investment goods as discussed above.

Further, the rise in fixed capital equipment in the period dt is equal to Jdt where J is the rate of excess of deliveries of fixed capital equipment over the required replacement R; and the negative influence upon the volume of new investment decisions in dt may be represented by $-bJdt$ where b is again a positive, but not necessarily a constant, coefficient. Thus, in so far as we would take into account only the factors enumerated above, we could write for the volume of new investment decisions in the period dt: $[R + (1 - c)(I - s)]dt + adP - bJdt$.[1]

4. We have not yet taken into account the influence of the rate of interest which must be deducted from the prospective rate of profit in order to obtain the net profitability. The rise in the rate of interest in the period dt will thus clearly reduce the volume of investment decisions in that period. This influence can be accounted for in the same way as prices of investment goods in the coefficient a, but because of the stability of the long-term rate of interest[2] as compared with the rate of profit it seems to be not very important.

We may thus consider as an approximate formula for new investment decisions $Rdt + (1 - c)(I - s)dt + adP - bJdt$. And the *rate* of investment decisions (both for replacement and extension), which we shall denote by D, may be obtained by dividing this expression by dt. We must yet, however, take into account that the phenomena inducing investment decisions do so with a certain time-lag which we may denote ω. We thus have

$$D_{t+\omega} = R_t + (1 - c)(I_t - s_t) + a\frac{dP_t}{dt} - bJ_t$$

or
$$D_{t+\omega} - R_t = a\frac{dP_t}{dt} - bJ_t + (1 - c)(I_t - s_t). \qquad . \quad (6)$$

It must be stressed that all the above argument applied to investment decisions with regard to fixed capital, and thus D

[1] This formula has a close affinity with that arrived at in my " Principle of Increasing Risk," *Economica*, November 1937, p. 447.   [2] Cf. pp. 39-40.

represents the rate of this type of decisions only. J is the net addition to fixed capital equipment, i.e. the difference between deliveries of finished fixed equipment over required replacement. I is the total net investment and consequently it differs from J in that it includes also the increase in working capital (*inter alia*, in fixed capital under construction) and stocks.

The coefficients a, b, and $1 - c$ are positive. In the extreme case when $b = 0$ and $1 - c = 0$ equation (6) would amount to saying that the excess of the rate of investment decisions over the level of maintenance and depreciation is proportionate (if a is constant) to the rate of change in profits. That would be nothing else but the so-called " acceleration principle " in the narrow sense which has been definitely disproved by statistical inquiries.[1] The acceleration principle requires that the rate of investment decisions is highest when profits (or output) pass through their medium position in the cycle on the way upwards. The facts, however, show that the maximum of investment decisions is reached in a much more advanced stage of the boom. This state of affairs may be accounted for by formula (6) if the coefficients b and $(1 - c)$ fulfil a certain condition. Indeed, if $1 - c > b$ one can say that investment decisions are, roughly speaking, in a double positive correlation with the rate of change of profits and the level of investment. (Real rentiers' savings s_t are rather stable in the course of the trade cycle.) Further, through the " multiplier equation " (see p. 60) profits are—with a short time-lag—positively correlated with investment. Thus the rate of investment decisions is in a double positive correlation with the rate of change in profits and the level of profits, and that means that it reaches its maximum somewhere between the medium position of recovery and the top of the boom.

5. It may easily be seen that in equation (6) is involved what one can call a " trend component." For it follows from it that long-run equilibrium of the system is impossible unless special assumptions are made about the rentiers' savings s. Indeed, in

---

[1] See, for instance, J. Tinbergen, " Critical Remarks on Some Business-Cycle Theories," *Econometrica*, April 1942.

a long-run equilibrium profits P are constant and net additions to fixed capital J and total net investment I are constant and $= 0$. The rate of gross investment decisions D is constant and $=$ required replacement R. Thus equation (6) becomes in such a state

$$0 = - (1 - c)s_t.$$

Consequently long-run equilibrium is possible only if the latter equation is fulfilled, which need not in general be the case because rentiers' savings s_t do not fall automatically to nought if net investment is at a zero level. If rentiers do some saving the system will thus be subject to a negative trend. Thus to obtain a model of the pure business cycle we assume for the present that in a business cycle period considered the rentiers do no saving so that $s = 0$. However, we shall re-introduce this factor in the last essay where we consider the problem of trend. For the purpose of discussion of the pure business cycle equation (6) is thus

$$D_{t+\omega} - R_t = a\frac{dP_t}{dt} - bJ_t + (1 - c)I_t. \qquad . \quad (6a)$$

Fundamental Equation for a Simplified Model

1. In addition to equation (6a) we have the following relations between the variables entering it.

There exists first a simple relation between the rate of investment decisions D and the deliveries of finished capital equipment. The rate of the latter follows the former with a time-lag θ which is equal to the average period of construction.

Thus to the rate of gross investment decisions $D_{t+\omega}$ in the last equation there corresponds an equal rate of deliveries at time $t + \omega + \theta$. As the latter is the sum of required replacement and of the net investment in fixed capital at the time $t + \omega + \theta$, we have

$$D_{t+\omega} = R_{t+\omega+\theta} + J_{t+\omega+\theta}.$$

Taking into consideration that required replacement varies slowly in time, and that the combined time-lag $\omega + \theta$ is rather small (something like a year), we may write as a good approximation

$$D_{t+\omega} - R_t = J_{t+\omega+\theta} \qquad . \qquad . \qquad . \quad (7)$$

where J is net investment in finished fixed capital (i.e. the excess of deliveries of finished fixed capital over the required replacement), the time-lag ω is related to the delay with which investment decisions are taken under the influence of inducements, and θ is the average construction period. From equations $(6a)$ and (7) we obtain

$$J_{t+\omega+\theta} = a\frac{dP_t}{dt} - bJ_t + (1 - c)I_t. \qquad . \quad (8)$$

2. As mentioned above I and J differ in that the latter represents the rate of net investment in finished fixed capital equipment only while I is the total rate of investment and thus includes the increase in working capital and stocks as well. Now while working capital rises with output stocks usually move in the opposite direction. As a first approximation we shall assume that these changes cancel each other and thus

$$I = J. \qquad . \qquad . \qquad . \quad (9)$$

A second approximation, based on a more general assumption about the movement of working capital and stocks, will be given at the end of the essay.

Taking into account equation (9) we obtain from equation (8)

$$I_{t+\omega+\theta} = a\frac{dP_t}{dt} + (1 - b - c)I_t, \qquad . \qquad . \quad (10)$$

and after subtracting from both sides I_t,

$$I_{t+\omega+\theta} - I_t = a\frac{dP_t}{dt} - (b + c)I_t.$$

If the change of I_t over a period $\omega + \theta$ may be assumed not far from linear, the difference $I_{t+\omega+\theta} - I_t$ may be represented as the derivative of the medium value $\dfrac{dI_{t+\frac{\omega+\theta}{2}}}{dt}$ multiplied by the length of the period $\omega + \theta$. If we denote $\omega + \theta$ by 2ϵ we thus have

$$I_{t+\omega+\theta} - I_t = 2\epsilon \frac{dI_{t+\epsilon}}{dt}$$

and equation (9) may be written

$$2\epsilon \frac{dI_{t+\epsilon}}{dt} = a\frac{dP_t}{dt} - (b + c)I_t. \qquad (10a)$$

If we integrate this equation (assuming that a, b and c are constants or functions of P_t and I_t respectively) we find that investment I is an increasing function of the real profits P and a decreasing one of the volume of capital equipment some time ago, which is the basis of the business cycle theory presented in my *Essays in the Theory of Economic Fluctuations*.

It should be noticed, however, that the significance of the integral of the negative member $-(b + c)I_t$ is now different from that which it had in my theory in the *Essays*. The negative influence of the level of investment I upon the increase in investment in the subsequent period in the equation (10a) expresses : (i) the adverse influence of the increase in capital equipment (coefficient b) ; (ii) the effect of entrepreneurs reinvesting only a part of their current savings, even though the objective determinants of the profitability of investment are unchanged (coefficient c). In my theory in the *Essays*, however, the latter factor was abstracted and thus c was assumed to be nought.

The present theory includes as special cases the " acceleration principle " theory ($b = 0$; $c = 1$; cf. p. 65) and my old theory ($c = 0$).

3. The equation (10a) expresses the change in investment as a function of the change in real profits and of the level of investment some time ago. But according to the " multiplier " equation (5) profits are in turn a function of investment with a time-lag

$$P_t = \frac{A_{t-\kappa} + I_{t-\kappa}}{1 - \lambda}. \qquad . \qquad . \qquad . \qquad (5)$$

From this follows, if the stable part of capitalists' consumption is assumed strictly constant for the " pure " business cycle discussion,

$$\frac{dP_t}{dt} = \frac{1}{1 - \lambda} \frac{dI_{t-\kappa}}{dt}. \qquad . \qquad . \qquad . \qquad (5a)$$

By substituting this value of $\frac{dP_t}{dt}$ into the equation (10a) we obtain the fundamental equation

$$2\epsilon \frac{dI_{t+\epsilon}}{dt} = \frac{a}{1 - \lambda} \frac{dI_{t-\kappa}}{dt} - (b + c)I_t$$

or
$$\frac{dI_{t+\epsilon+\kappa}}{dt} = \frac{a}{2\epsilon(1 - \lambda)} \frac{dI_t}{dt} - \frac{b + c}{2\epsilon} I_{t+\kappa}. \qquad . \qquad (11)$$

This equation tells us that with a given a the change in investment to-day induces a proportionate change after a time $\epsilon + \kappa$ which, however, will be retarded by the positive level of investment I in the intermediate period ($t + \kappa$ lies between t and $t + \epsilon + \kappa$); while if this item is negative its influence will be accelerating.

The retarding influence of I reflects : (i) the adverse effect of the increase in capital equipment upon the rate of profit (co-efficient b); (ii) the consequences of the fact that entrepreneurs reinvest only a part of their current savings even though the objective determinants of the profitability of investment are unchanged (coefficient c).

The Mechanism of the Business Cycle

1. Let us now divide the time into periods equal to the time-lag $\epsilon + \kappa$. The points 0, 1, 2 . . . in Figure 6 show the rate of real net investment I in successive " unit periods." (The horizontal distance between two successive points is $\epsilon + \kappa$.) The rate of change from one unit period to another is then given by the inclination of the segments 0-1, 1-2, etc. It follows directly from equation (11) that the change in the period 0-1, induces that in 1-2 ; the change 1-2 induces in turn that in 2-3, etc., and that the coefficient of this influence is $\frac{a}{2\epsilon(1 - \lambda)}$. When dis-

cussing the process we must, of course, take into account: (1) variations in the coefficient *a* which measures the strength of the influence of the change in real profits upon investment and is *not* constant; (2) the retarding influence of the rate of net investment *I* when it is positive or its accelerating influence when it is negative. It follows from the equation (11) that the time-lag between the influence of *I* and the corresponding change in the rate of investment is ϵ. If one remembers that the periods 0-1, 1-2, etc., are of the length $\epsilon + \kappa$ the relevant *I* for the change of investment in the period 1-2 is somewhere between the middle

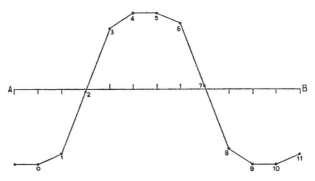

FIG. 6.—Hypothetical Time-Curve of Net Investment.
(A-B corresponds to zero net investment.)

of 0-1 and 1-2, for the change in investment in the period 2-3 somewhere between the middle of 1-2 and 2-3, etc.

2. Let us start our discussion of the mechanism of the business cycle from point 1 being the end of the period 0-1 in which a moderate recovery from the bottom of the slump has taken place. The positive change in investment in 0-1 induces a positive change in 1-2. The coefficient *a* may be assumed here very high. The entrepreneurs know that "the recovery is on." The change in profits is therefore an inducement to them not only because the rate of profit as calculated on the basis of current profits has increased, but also because they anticipate a further considerable rise in profits in the near future. Further, the relevant net investment *I* is negative here, which contributes to the increase in

the rate of change in 1-2 as compared with 0-1. As a result the rise in investment in the period 1-2 is considerably larger than in the period 0-1.

In the subsequent period a will fall sharply because the anticipations of entrepreneurs about a *further* rise in profits in the near future will be less optimistic : they have already a part of the boom behind them. This and the retarding influence of the positive I will finally reduce the rate of change. This need not, however, necessarily happen already in the period 2-3. If $\dfrac{a}{2\epsilon(1-\lambda)}$ for the period 1-2 was much higher than 1, then even after a has fallen considerably it may produce in 2-3 a greater or equal change in investment to that in 1-2. (On our graph it is assumed to be equal.) But after some time the rate of change in investment will slacken. (On the graph it is assumed to have happened in the period 3-4.) This leads finally to the stop of the rise in investment (on the graph in the period 4-5).

In the subsequent period 5-6 the rate of investment must begin to fall. For the change in investment 4-5 was nought, which without the influence of I would mean a stationary level of investment in 5-6 ; but the net addition to fixed capital equipment and the incomplete reinvestment of entrepreneurs' savings [1] cause a *reduction* in investment in 5-6.

Now the " slump is on " and a for the subsequent period 6-7 is very high because the entrepreneurs discount the *further* fall in profits in the near future while I is still positive, which accelerates the slump. The gradual reduction in a as these anticipations lose in strength and the negative value of I slackens the rate of fall in investment and finally brings it to a standstill in the period 9-10.

Next the negative I extricates the system from the slump just as its positive value made for the turning-point in the boom. We have thus a moderate recovery in the subsequent 10-11 which starts the boom in the next period as described above.

[1] The importance of the " incomplete reinvestment " factor for the explanation of the turning-point in the boom was emphasized for the first time by E. Rothbarth in a lecture to the Economic Society of the London School of Economics in 1939.

3. In this description of the mechanism of the business cycle we have left out of consideration the factor of changes in prices of investment goods. As mentioned above (p. 63), these should be accounted for in the variations of the coefficient a. The greater the change in the prices of investment goods accompanying the change in real profits dP the smaller a. It follows that in the advanced stage of the boom when raw materials and wages in investment goods industries rise rather sharply, a is likely to be reduced by this factor and so to contribute another reason for its fall from the high level it has at the beginning of the recovery.

The bottleneck in the existing capacities in investment goods industries may also contribute to the rise of prices of investment goods and thus hamper the advance of investment. Here, however, an even more important factor may be the " stretching " of orders, which will work as follows. The time-lag between investment orders and deliveries θ will increase and so, as a result, will the time-lag $\epsilon = \dfrac{\omega + \theta}{2}$ (ω is the delay in the influence of " inducements to invest " upon investment decisions). As the coefficient of influence of the change in investment in a " unit period " upon that in the next unit period is $\dfrac{a}{2\epsilon(1 - \lambda)}$, the rise in ϵ contributes to slowing down the increase of investment in the same way as the fall in a considered above.

It must be added that in the advanced stage of the boom investment decisions may be discouraged by the difficulty of finding suitable labour for employment in the new plant. This may be also accounted for in our scheme by the fall in the coefficient a. This factor will prevent investment from rising to the level at which full employment in the strict sense is reached.

4. The period of the trade cycle as described above depends on the time-lag $\epsilon + \kappa$ and on the values of the coefficients $\dfrac{a}{2\epsilon(1 - \lambda)}$ and $\dfrac{b + c}{2\epsilon}$ in the course of the trade cycle. One can say roughly that with a given time-lag $\epsilon + \kappa$ the cycle is the shorter (1) the more sharply a falls with the increasing level of

profits in the boom or with the decreasing level of profits in the slump; (2) the stronger the rise or fall in the rate of investment decisions at the beginning of the boom or slump (periods 1-2 and 6-7); (3) the higher the coefficient $\dfrac{b + c}{2\epsilon}$. For all these factors tend to shorten the duration of the boom and slump, and thus the period of the business cycle. (If $b = 0$ and $c = 0$ there would be no fall at all from the high level reached in the boom nor a rise from the low level reached in the slump.)

An important point about any trade cycle theory is whether the cycle may be damped down or not. Indeed, the course of the cyclical fluctuations as determined by the fundamental equation may be such that the amplitude diminishes from cycle to cycle so that the system gradually approaches a state of equilibrium. It is true that it has been shown that a combination of a damping mechanism with erratic shocks (due to the fact that the economic relations as represented by the fundamental equation are rather loose) produces cycles with an amplitude which has no tendency to decline.[1] But if damping is strong such cyclical movements would be of extremely irregular character. Thus, because it is difficult to prove why the coefficients of the fundamental equation should be such as to exclude strong damping, these theories have a serious loophole.[2] Our present theory is free of this difficulty. It may be shown that the type of variations assumed for the co-efficient a prevents the cycle from being damped down.

In the period 1-2 after the beginning of recovery in 0-1 $\dfrac{a}{2\epsilon(1 - \lambda)}$ is much greater than 1, and this accelerates the rise of investment in 1-2. If, however, the recovery in 0-1 was slight, the increase in investment in the period 1-2 may be not very considerable in spite of a high a. But then the entrepreneurs have not much of the boom behind them and therefore a does not fall strongly, and $\dfrac{a}{2\epsilon(1 - \lambda)}$ still remains greater than 1. Thus

---

[1] Professor Frisch, "Propagation Problems and Impulse Problems in Dynamics," *Economic Essays in Honour of Gustav Cassel*, London 1933, and unpublished work.

[2] This may also be said of my theory in the *Essays*, see p. 148.

the acceleration in the rise of investment continues, and so a high level of investment is reached. Then, however, $\dfrac{a}{2\epsilon(1 - \lambda)}$ does fall below 1, the increase of investment is slowed down and finally is brought to a standstill (by this variation of a and by the retarding influence of the positive I, i.e. by the rise in fixed capital equipment and incomplete reinvestment of entrepreneurs' savings). From this description it is clear that investment must rise appreciably above the zero line A-B because it is only at a relatively advanced stage of the boom that $\dfrac{a}{2\epsilon(1 - \lambda)}$ declines considerably below 1.

The amplitude of the cycle depends, therefore, chiefly on the level of investment at which $\dfrac{a}{2\epsilon(1 - \lambda)}$ begins to fall below 1, on how strongly it falls with the further rise of investment, and also on the coefficient $\dfrac{b + c}{2\epsilon}$ which measures the intensity of the retarding influence of the level of I. The higher the level of investment at which $\dfrac{a}{2\epsilon(1 - \lambda)}$ begins to fall below 1, the slower it falls with the further rise of investment, and the smaller the coefficient $\dfrac{b + c}{2\epsilon}$ the higher the amplitude.[1]

5. One query must still be answered. Our business cycle mechanism seems to imply that there is always recovery from a slump. On the other hand, it has been shown in the essay on

---

[1] With regard to the fact that the business cycle cannot be damped down and its amplitude is determined by the parameters of the system, the above theory has a certain affinity to that of Mr. Kaldor (*Economic Journal*, March 1940). He obtained his results by examining a special case of my theory in the *Essays* which I have failed to consider. His theory is therefore based on the assumption of a particular shape of the functional relation between income and the rate of investment decisions ; and it is difficult to advance any satisfactory *a priori* reasons for this shape's being necessarily such as he assumes. In my present theory the cycle is prevented from being damped down by variations in a (the coefficient of the influence of profits upon the rate of investment decisions), and the pattern of these changes in variations seems to me much better founded than the shape of Mr. Kaldor's curve.

the theory of profits that investment activity can persist over long periods at its minimum level. How can this apparent contradiction be reconciled? The answer is that a situation is conceivable in which the factors causing a recovery from the slump in our business cycle model will prove inadequate.

With a given rate of interest—and the long-term rate of interest cannot fall below a certain minimum (see p. 58)—there will always be a level of the rate of profit at which all investment activity (both extensions and replacements except for necessary repairs) will stop because no investment plan appears profitable. If the rate of profit is at this level or below it, the rate of investment is at its minimum.

Imagine now that in a slump I has reached its minimum level I_{min}. According to our formula (5) we may write for profits in this situation

$$P = \frac{A + I_{min}}{1 - \lambda}.$$

Moreover, assume that the value of the stable part of capitalists' consumption in relation to the volume of capital equipment is such that the rate of profit is then appreciably *below* the level at which all investment plans become unprofitable. It is easy to show that the system is then unlikely to extricate itself from the slump. True, the volume of capital shrinks with lapse of time because depreciation is not made good, and thus the rate of profit increases because A is assumed here to be constant. But this rise is very slow, and it will take a number of years before the level of the rate of profit is reached at which any investment plans begin to become profitable. In such a situation, however, the assumption that A is constant cannot be upheld any more : the capitalists' " standard of living " will be adversely affected by the protracted slump and thus the system is likely never to reach the position where investment would start to recover from its minimum level.

6. So far we have dealt only with the fluctuations in net investment I. But since net " real " profits P are connected with I by equation (5),

$$P_t = \frac{A + I_{t-\kappa}}{1 - \lambda},$$

their fluctuations follow those of net investment.   And as the
required replacement R fluctuates only slightly in the course of the
trade cycle, the changes in gross profits $P + R$ are also roughly
determined by those in net investment I.   Further, the fluctuations in the national output will be determined by those in gross
real profits and by factors determining the distribution of the
gross national income (cf. p. 50).   However, the fluctuations in
distribution are much smaller than those in gross profit $P + R$,
and therefore output moves in the same direction as $P + R$.

The factors which cause a relative shift from gross profits to
other incomes in the slump and from other incomes to gross
profits in the boom tend to reduce the amplitude of output
fluctuations, and conversely.   For instance, if the salary bill rises
relative to gross profits in the slump this tends to mitigate the
decline in output.   The fall in the ratio of material costs to wage
costs in the slump tends to raise the relative share of wages in the
national income (cf. p. 17) and thus works in the same direction.
But the rise in the degree of oligopoly in a deep slump tends to
reduce the relative share of wages in the national income (cf. p. 18)
and thus to accentuate the fall in output.

The Problem of Stocks and Working Capital

1. All our argument so far has been based on the very special
assumption that changes in working capital and stocks cancel
each other.   We shall now introduce a more general hypothesis.

Let us recall that before making any assumption about the
movement of working capital and stocks we arrived on page 67
at the equation

$$J_{t+\omega+\theta} = a\frac{dP_t}{dt} - bJ_t + (\mathbf{1} - c)I_t. \qquad . \qquad . \qquad (8)$$

Now, however, we do *not* assume that total investment I is equal
to the investment in finished fixed capital J, which is equivalent
to changes in working capital being always just offset by that
in stocks.   Instead we shall assume that the balance of these
influences is proportionate to the derivative of profits dP/dt; this
is justified by the fact that the increase in working capital and the

running down of stocks are caused by the increase in output, the movement of which is closely correlated with that of profits (see p. 76). We thus say that the change in working capital and stocks at time t is $e\dfrac{dP_t}{dt}$.[1]

The coefficient e (not necessarily a constant) is positive if the increase in working capital is less than offset by the running down of stocks and negative if it is more than offset by it. Statistical data suggests that it is the former case which is of practical importance. Now as the total investment I_t is equal to that in finished fixed capital J_t + the change in working capital and stocks, we have

$$I_t - J_t = e\frac{dP_t}{dt}, \qquad . \qquad . \qquad . \quad (12)$$

and from this and the equation (8) we obtain

$$I_{t+\omega+\theta} - e\frac{dP_{t+\omega+\theta}}{dt} = a\frac{dP_t}{dt} - b\Big(I_t - e\frac{dP_t}{dt}\Big) + (1 - c)I_t,$$

or $\quad I_{t+\omega+\theta} - I_t = (a + be)\dfrac{dP_t}{dt} + e\dfrac{dP_{t+\omega+\theta}}{dt} - (b + c)I_t.$

After adding and subtracting $e\dfrac{dP_t}{dt}$ on the right-hand side we have

$$I_{t+\omega+\theta} - I_t = (a + be + e)\frac{dP_t}{dt} + e\Big(\frac{dP_{t+\omega+\theta}}{dt} - \frac{dP_t}{dt}\Big) - (b + c)I_t.$$

By applying the transformation described on pp. 67-68 to $I_{t+\omega+\theta} - I_t$ and to $\dfrac{dP_{t+\omega+\theta}}{dt} - \dfrac{dP_t}{dt}$ and denoting $\dfrac{\omega + \theta}{2} = \epsilon,\ a + be + e = a'$ we obtain

$$2\epsilon\frac{dI_{t+\epsilon}}{dt} = a'\frac{dP_t}{dt} + 2\epsilon e\frac{d^2P_{t+\epsilon}}{dt^2} - (b + c)I_t. \qquad . \quad (13)$$

---

[1] There may be involved here a short time-lag which we leave out of consideration for the sake of simplicity ; this does not affect significantly the results of our subsequent argument.

Further, we have the " multiplier equation " for profits

$$\frac{dP_t}{dt} = \frac{1}{1 - \lambda} \frac{dI_{t-\kappa}}{dt}. \qquad \qquad (5a)$$

After substitution of this value of $\frac{dP_t}{dt}$ into equation (13) we arrive at

$$2\epsilon \frac{dI_{t+\epsilon}}{dt} = \frac{a'}{1 - \lambda} \frac{dI_{t-\kappa}}{dt} + \frac{2\epsilon e}{1 - \lambda} \frac{d^2 I_{t+\epsilon-\kappa}}{dt^2} - (b + c)I_t,$$

or $\quad \frac{dI_{t+\epsilon+\kappa}}{dt} = \frac{a'}{2\epsilon(1 - \lambda)} \frac{dI_t}{dt} + \frac{e}{1 - \lambda} \frac{d^2 I_{t+\epsilon}}{dt^2} - \frac{b + c}{2\epsilon} I_{t+\kappa}. \quad (14)$

2. This equation differs from the equation (11)—obtained on the basis of the special assumption of the changes in working capital and in stocks cancelling each other—only by the member $\frac{e}{1 - \lambda} \frac{d^2 I_{t+\epsilon}}{dt^2}$ and by a' having a different significance from a $(a' = a + be + e)$. The business cycle mechanism described above was based on the fact that—according to the equation (11) —given the coefficient a and $b + c$, the rate of change of investment $\frac{dI_{t+\epsilon+\kappa}}{dt}$ is an increasing linear function of the rate of change of investment some time ago $\frac{dI_t}{dt}$, and a diminishing one of the level of investment in between, $I_{t+\kappa}$. (There were also made some plausible assumptions about the variation of the coefficient a.) At present the rate of change of investment $\frac{dI_{t+\epsilon+\kappa}}{dt}$ is in addition an increasing linear function of $\frac{d^2 I_{t+\epsilon}}{dt^2}$, i.e. of the acceleration of the increase in investment in between $(t + \epsilon$ lies between t and $t + \epsilon + \kappa$). It follows that the acceleration of the increase in investment at the beginning of recovery in our mechanism and its slowing down in the advanced stage will now be accentuated because $\frac{d^2 I_{t+\epsilon}}{dt^2}$ will be positive in the first stage and negative

in the second one. At the top of the boom $\dfrac{d^2 I_{t+\varepsilon}}{dt^2}$ will be negative
and will thus contribute to the breakdown of the boom alongside
with the adverse influence of the positive investment (member
$-\dfrac{b+c}{2\epsilon} I_{t+\kappa}$). The position in the downward movement
and at the bottom of the slump is symmetrical. Thus the
pattern of the business cycle is not fundamentally changed by
our new hypothesis about the changes in working capital and
stocks.[1]

It must be stressed that even our second approximation to the
movement of working capital and stocks is still very far from
giving an accurate picture of the processes in question. From
the scanty information we have, changes in working capital and
stocks are much too complex to be accounted for by a simple
formula. But it is likely that the deviations of the actual state of
affairs from our second approximation are not sufficiently important to require fundamental changes in our pattern of the
business cycle.

[1] This, however, is subject to a certain qualification. The member $\dfrac{e}{1-\lambda}\dfrac{d^2 I_{t+\varepsilon}}{dt^2}$
and the fact that $a' = a + be + e$ may cause, if e is not sufficiently low, the boom
(or slump) in investment to continue in spite of the fall in the coefficient a and the
retarding influence of the member $-\dfrac{b+c}{2\epsilon} I_{t+\kappa}$.

With regard to the *boom*, however, it may be shown that in this case a stage
is finally reached where e falls to a very low level. Indeed the rate of change of
working capital and stocks has been assumed $= e\dfrac{dP}{dt}$ because it is positively correlated with the change in output, and this in turn is positively correlated with the
change in real profits P. Now if the system approaches the state of full employment the national output almost ceases to grow, even though investment and
profits continue to rise. As a result the increase in working capital and stocks
almost stops as well and thus e must fall to a very low level.

The argument does not apply to the *slump*, and here a sufficiently high level of
e *could* cause a downswing of a cumulative character.

5. THE TREND

General Remarks on Trend

1. We shall now discuss the influence of factors which were abstracted in the preceding essay in order to obtain a " pure " business cycle in a trendless economy. We must, however, first deal shortly with the general problem of trend in relation to our " business cycle equation " :

$$\frac{dI_{t+\theta+\kappa}}{dt} = \frac{a}{2\epsilon(1-\lambda)} \frac{dI_t}{dt} - \frac{b+c}{2\epsilon} I_{t+\kappa}. \qquad (11)$$

(For the sake of simplicity we take as a basis of our inquiry into the problem of trend the equation which involves the assumption that the volume of working capital and stocks is constant. By this we abstract from the influence of the long-run changes in working capital and stocks upon the development of the system. This may be justified as a first approximation on the ground that in long-run development changes in working capital and stocks play a subordinate rôle as compared with the accumulation of fixed capital.)

Suppose that as a result of the preceding long-run development of the economy there will appear on the right hand of the above equation an additional member $L(t)$,

$$\frac{dI_{t+\theta+\kappa}}{dt} = \frac{a}{2\epsilon(1-\lambda)} \frac{dI_t}{dt} - \frac{b+c}{2\epsilon} I_{t+\kappa} + L(t), \qquad (15)$$

and thus the rate of change of investment $\frac{dI_{t+\theta+\kappa}}{dt}$ will have an additional determinant depending on the preceding evolution of the system. If such is the case the economy cannot be trendless any more. Moreover, this current trend, being the result of the preceding developments, contributes in turn to the future long-run development of the economy. It is in this way that a long-run dynamic process arises. We shall next examine briefly the influence of the features of the function $L(t)$ upon the character of the trend.

2. Let us assume first that over the period considered $L(t)$ is a constant which we shall denote by L. Our equation is then

$$\frac{dI_{t+\varepsilon+\kappa}}{dt} = \frac{a}{2\varepsilon(1-\lambda)}\frac{dI_t}{dt} - \frac{b+c}{2\varepsilon}I_{t+\kappa} + L. \qquad (15a)$$

Imagine now that over a certain business cycle the average of the rate of investment I is I_0 and that this value fulfils the condition

$$\frac{b+c}{2\varepsilon}I_0 = L. \qquad . \qquad . \qquad (16)$$

Let us further denote the deviations of I from its average by I' so that we have

$$I = I_0 + I'.$$

By substituting this value into the equation $(15a)$ and taking into account the equation (16) we obtain

$$\frac{dI'_{t+\varepsilon+\kappa}}{dt} = \frac{a}{2\varepsilon(1-\lambda)}\frac{dI'_t}{dt} - \frac{b+c}{2\varepsilon}I'_{t+\kappa}. \qquad (17)$$

This equation means the same with regard to I' as equation (11) meant with regard to I. It follows that I' fluctuates now round the level I_0 in the same way as in the case of the " pure " business cycle it fluctuates round zero.

Now it may be seen that this is *the* solution of the business cycle and trend problem when $L(t)$ is a constant. Indeed, let us assume that the average of I over the cycle period, I_0, does *not* fulfil the condition (16). Imagine, for instance, that

$$\frac{b+c}{2\varepsilon}I_0 < L.$$

Then, as it is easy to see, equation (17) would contain a positive trend component $L - \dfrac{b+c}{2\varepsilon}I_0$. But that would mean that the average of I' over the cycle period could not be zero, and thus the average of I would be *not* equal to I_0. It follows that I_0 must fulfil the condition (16).

Consequently, if L is constant and positive, the rate of investment after elimination of the business cycle is positive (as $b + c > 0$) and stable. Capital accumulates but the rate of investment does not rise. If $L(t)$ is an increasing function the rate of investment also increases in the long run, while it falls if $L(t)$ is a decreasing function. Positive long-run investment may be thus rising, stable, or falling. The rising trend in the volume of capital need not be accompanied by a similar trend in the rate of investment. Statistics of net investment in fixed capital in

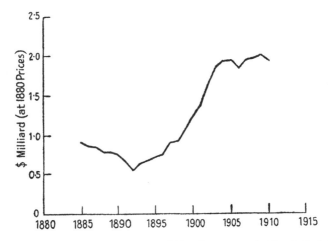

FIG. 7.—Nine-Year Moving Average of Net Investment in Fixed Capital (except Dwelling Houses) in the U.S.A. at 1880 Prices, 1881-1914 (Source: Professor Douglas, *The Theory of Wages*, p. 465).

the U.S.A. in the period 1881-1914 show a very good example of this state of affairs (see Fig. 7).

3. As long-run expansion of capital equipment may be accompanied by a fall in the rate of net investment, it is also uncertain whether net profits P will rise with the accumulation of capital. Indeed, according to equation (5), $P_t = \dfrac{A_{t-\kappa} + I_{t-\kappa}}{1 - \lambda}$ and thus, if I falls, P increases only if the stable part of capitalists' consumption A rises sufficiently to offset the decrease in I. The

gross profits $P + R$ have a greater chance to rise with the expansion of capital equipment than the net profits P, because the required replacement R rises in the long run more or less proportionately to the stock of capital. (For the same reason gross investment $I + R$ has a greater chance to rise with the volume of capital equipment than net investment I.)

The position of the salary bill is similar to that of required replacement. It will usually tend to increase with the volume of capital equipment. For this reason net profits + required replacement + salaries, i.e. profits + overheads, have a much greater chance to increase in their real value with the rise of the volume of capital equipment than net profits P.

Finally, the changes in the wage bill will be determined by changes in profits + overheads and in factors determining the distribution of the gross national income. For instance the long-run rise in the degree of oligopoly will make the wage bill fall relative to other incomes.

It follows from the above that it is not quite certain whether the gross national income or national output will increase in the long run with capital equipment. But, if there is no important change in the relative share of wages in the gross national income, such an increase is in any case much more likely than that in net profits. For the expansion in capital equipment tends to increase overheads (depreciation and maintenance, and the salary bill). And with no important changes in the relative share of wages the national output changes more or less proportionately to profits + overheads.

Long-Run Changes in Capitalists' Consumption

1. On page 60 we assumed, for the sake of the " pure business cycle " discussion, that the stable part of capitalists' consumption A_t is a constant, although in fact it varies slowly in time as a result of preceding long-run development which has influenced the capitalists' standard of living. We shall now remove this assumption and thus we must take into account that dA_t/dt is not in general equal to zero.

On page 69 we obtained from the formula

$$P_t = \frac{A_{t-\kappa} + I_{t-\kappa}}{1 - \lambda}$$

the derivative of profits

$$\frac{dP_t}{dt} = \frac{1}{1 - \lambda} \frac{dI_{t-\kappa}}{dt}$$

under the assumption that A is constant. If $\frac{dA}{dt} \neq 0$ we have

$$\frac{dP_t}{dt} = \frac{1}{1 - \lambda}\left(\frac{dA_{t-\kappa}}{dt} + \frac{dI_{t-\kappa}}{dt}\right).$$

It may be easily found from the argument on page 69 that as a result an additional member $\dfrac{a}{2\epsilon(1 - \lambda)} \dfrac{dA_t}{dt}$ will appear on the right hand of the equation (11). In other words, we have here a trend component

$$L(t) = \frac{a}{2\epsilon(1 - \lambda)} \frac{dA_t}{dt}.{}^1$$

2. The trend component is here positive if $\dfrac{dA_t}{dt} > 0$, because the coefficient $\dfrac{a}{2\epsilon(1 - \lambda)}$ is positive. Thus, according to the results arrived at in the last section, a positive change in the stable part of capitalists' consumption causes a long-run accumulation of capital. This is quite plausible because a positive dA/dt means a positive trend in profits P because $P_t = \dfrac{1}{1 - \lambda}(A_{t-\kappa} + I_{t-\kappa})$. A system which we rendered stationary in the essay on " pure

---

¹ The problem is actually a little more complicated because of the fact that the coefficient a undergoes cyclical fluctuations. However, a may be represented as $a_0 + a'$, where a_0 is the average a over the cycle period and a' the deviation of a from a_0. Thus $\dfrac{a}{2\epsilon(1 - \lambda)} \dfrac{dA_t}{dt} = \dfrac{a_0}{2\epsilon(1 - \lambda)} \dfrac{dA_t}{dt} + \dfrac{a'}{2\epsilon(1 - \lambda)} \dfrac{dA_t}{dt}$. The actual trend component is $\dfrac{a_0}{2\epsilon(1 - \lambda)} \dfrac{dA_t}{dt}$. The member $\dfrac{a'}{2\epsilon(1 - \lambda)} \dfrac{dA_t}{dt}$ is of cyclical character ; it will have a certain influence upon the course of the trade cycle.

business cycle " by the assumption that $\dfrac{dA}{dt} = 0$ will be an expanding one—at least with regard to capital equipment—if dA/dt is positive.

Now what factors in the past long-run development cause the rise (or fall) of the stable part of capitalists' consumption A ? A secular rise in wealth and income of capitalists tends to raise, with rather a long time-lag, their " standard of living," i.e. the amount they are apt to consume irrespective of the level of their current income. Thus an increase in capital and profits in the past tends to cause a positive dA/dt. But these are not the only factors in question. For the long-run rise in capital and profits may be associated with the concentration of both, and this tends to reduce A.

It follows that the trend caused by a positive dA/dt in a certain period need not be " self-continuing." True, a positive dA/dt causes an accumulation of capital which tends to cause A to increase in the future. It is, however, not certain if a positive dA_t/dt causes a rise in profits [1] which are the other link with the future changes in A. Moreover, the possible increase in the concentration of capitalists' wealth and income may induce a fall in A even though capital and profits were rising over the past long period.

Rentiers' Savings

1. To render our system trendless we also abstracted from rentiers' savings (see p. 66). If they are taken into consideration it follows from page 64 and the subsequent argument (pp. 66-69) that an additional member $-\dfrac{1-c}{2\epsilon}s_{t+\kappa}$ appears on the right-hand side of equation (11). We have thus a trend component,

$$L(t) = -\frac{1-c}{2\epsilon}s_{t+\kappa},$$

[1] We have for them the formula $P = \dfrac{A_{t-\kappa} + I_{t-\kappa}}{1-\lambda}$. Now if $\dfrac{dA}{dt}$ is positive so is the long-run rate of investment, but as shown in the preceding section, I may be constant, rising or falling. And thus in the latter case it is not certain that the profits P rise even though A increases.

where $s_{t+\kappa}$ is the "real" value of rentiers' savings. $L(t)$ is here always negative. Indeed, the coefficient $1 - c$ is positive (see p. 63); so, of course, is the time-lag ϵ, and the real rentiers' saving may be assumed always to be positive because their real incomes are rather steady (except in abnormal cases of hyper-inflation), and on the average sufficiently large to make them savers. Consequently, according to the preceding section, the existence of rentiers' savings causes a negative long-run invest-ment, i.e. long-run shrinking of capital equipment. This is not surprising. By the assumption $s = 0$ we obtained in the essay on the "pure business cycle" a trendless system. But such a stationary situation (from the long-run point of view) is incom-patible with positive rentiers' savings because this causes a con-tinuous increase in the entrepreneurs' indebtedness towards rentiers which depresses investment activity (cf. pp. 61-62). Therefore the rentiers' savings—if taken in isolation from other trend factors—create a negative trend.

2. If prices are falling over a certain long period it causes the real value of rentiers' savings to increase over this period and thus accelerates the negative trend caused by them. If, because of the existence of positive trend factors, the total $L(t)$ is positive, the long-run fall in prices tends to decrease $L(t)$. But, as shown in the preceding section, a decreasing $L(t)$ causes a long-run fall in the rate of net investment I. It follows that the long-run fall in prices will, through this channel, affect adversely the long-run rate of net investment.

The Rise in Population and the Increasing Productivity of Labour

1. It is frequently maintained that the main reason for trend is the rise in population or the increase in productivity due to technical progress. No doubt one or the other is a *necessary* condition for a long-run expansion of output of an economy which has no large reserve army of unemployed. But are they also a *sufficient* condition? Does the rise in population or the increase in labour productivity due to technical progress *induce* the trend movement?

Let us first consider the influence of the rise in population. If population increases while output remains stable in the long-run there will be a secular increase in unemployment. This exerts a pressure on money wages which consequently tend to fall. The problem is thus reduced to the question : How will a long-run fall in money wages affect our trend analysis ? Now money wages do not appear at all in our fundamental equations. That may be traced to the fact that real profits P are fully determined by past consumption and investment decisions of capitalists and that into their current decisions enter again current real profits and the volume of capital equipment (or changes in these elements). This is in line with the Keynesian theory of money wages. There is, however, one influence of money wages which should enter our fundamental equation and was abstracted only for our " pure business cycle " analysis. Indeed, a long-run fall in money wages causes a fall in prices and thus with stable output a fall in the money volume of transactions. If the supply of cash by banks is not proportionately reduced this leads in turn to a long-run fall of the short-term rate of interest which results in a fall of the long-term rate of interest. Now such a fall will make for the appearance of a positive member $L(t)$ on the right-hand side of our fundamental equation and cause a positive trend movement. The increase in output in such a movement cannot, however, be so great as to prevent the long-run increase in unemployment for in such a case the very cause of the trend would disappear.

2. Let us now consider the effects of the increase in the productivity of labour due to technical progress. The immediate effect, as in the case of a wage cut, is to reduce wage costs and prices. This causes a fall in turnover (money volume of transactions) and consequently a decline in the rate of interest, which creates a tendency for a positive trend. If as a result output increases in the same proportion as productivity of labour, no unemployment arises.

If, however, the increase in output is smaller, " technological unemployment " must appear. This (as in the case of the increase in population) will depress wages. As a result an additional fall in the rate of interest will ensue which will induce an additional positive trend. But the latter cannot lead to a full absorption of "technological unemployment" for then the very cause of the additional trend would cease to exist.

3. The functioning of the mechanisms described seems, however, to be of very doubtful character. The connection between the rise in unemployment and the fall of money wages is rather loose if strong trade unions are in existence. Even more uncertain is the connection between the fall in turnover and that in the short-term rate of interest in the long run. If the fall in turnover continues over a long period the banking policy may easily adapt itself to this secular fall in such a way that the supply of balances shrinks *pari passu* with turnover and thus no fall in the short-term rate of interest occurs. In any case if growth of population and increase in productivity of labour were the main causes of trend the turnover would have a secular tendency to fall, which is by no means generally the case. Moreover, as we have seen in the last section, the secular fall in the price level exerts a negative influence upon the expansion of the economy by increasing the real value of rentiers' saving, and this counteracts the positive effect of the pressing down of the rate of interest.

To conclude : although growth of population or increasing productivity are a necessary condition for the long-run expansion of output if no large reserves of labour are available, these factors seem not to play an important rôle in *inducing* the trend movement.[1]

---

[1] It is sometimes maintained that the increase in population encourages investment because the entrepreneurs anticipate a broadening market. What is important, however, in this context is not the increase in population but in purchasing power. The increase in the number of paupers does not broaden the market. For instance, increased population does not mean necessarily a higher demand for houses : without an increase in the purchasing power the result may well be crowding of more people into the existing dwelling space. On the other hand, it should be noticed that our conclusions are valid only if our simplifying assumptions that the system is closed and the State Budget balanced are fulfilled. In an open system the fall in wage rates resulting from unemployment growing as a result of the increase in population will stimulate exports and so contribute to the upward trend. The payment of doles for unemployed, if financed by Government borrowing, will constitute another channel through which the rise in population may cause a positive trend of the system.

It follows that growing population and increasing productivity of labour may well cause long-run unemployment without setting to work forces which would absorb it.

Innovations

1. We tried to show above that the increase in productivity of labour due to technical progress is not likely *as such* to be an important factor in creating a trend movement. This does not mean, however, that technical progress as a whole is an indifferent phenomenon in this respect. On the contrary, some aspects of technical progress, we mean innoviations, *are* probably one of the main forces behind the long-run economic development.

The influence of new inventions upon investment consists in making the profitability of a certain type of investment higher than it would be otherwise. A new invention will therefore be another factor—alongside the change in current profits and capital equipment (see pp. 63-64)—which causes the emergence of investment decisions in a given period. With the replacement of old equipment by modern, the additional profitability of investment caused by the invention is gradually reduced and this has a negative effect upon investment decisions. The appearance of new inventions has a similar effect in the sphere of investment activity as a rise in current profits ; the repercussions of the " spreading " of inventions by replacing old by modern equipment may be compared with those of a fall in current profits.

Thus in any period we have the positive influence of new inventions on the one hand, and the negative effect of the gradual " liquidation " of past ones on the other. We shall call the technical progress uniform with regard to investment if these two effects upon an economy of a given size cancel out. If the effect is on balance positive or negative, we shall speak of accelerated or retarded technical progress.

2. It may seem from the definition of uniform technical progress that the corresponding trend component $L(t) = 0$ because the effect of new inventions on investment are exactly

offset by the "liquidation" of past ones. That may be so, but need not necessarily be the case.

We stressed in our definition that the positive and negative effect cancel out with regard to an economy of a *given size*. Now the larger the economy the larger is the positive effect of new inventions upon investment ; it may be considered roughly proportionate to the volume of capital equipment. Further, the negative effect of replacements "liquidating" the old inventions may be assumed roughly proportionate to the volume of old equipment at the time when the respective inventions emerged. It follows clearly that if we have a uniform technical progress, but if in the longer period preceding the period considered the equipment was steadily growing, the positive effect will be larger than the negative effect, i.e. $L(t) > 0$. And only in the case when the equipment was stationary in the preceding long period is $L(t) = 0$. Thus uniform technical progress will cause the development of the preceding long period to continue ; for, as shown above, a positive trend component $L(t)$ causes a long-run accumulation of capital. While, if the system was stationary in the preceding long period, uniform technical progress will not induce expansion because then $L(t) = 0$.

A stationary economy is thus not incompatible with uniform technical progress. But if the economy expanded prior to the period considered, the uniform technical progress will cause this expansion to continue.

3. In the latter case the positive trend component $L(t)$ depends on two factors : (1) It is the greater the larger is the rate of capital accumulation, i.e. of net investment, in the preceding long-run period, because the stronger was the preceding expansion the greater the difference between the positive effect of new inventions and the negative effect of the liquidation of past inventions. (2) In addition $L(t)$ depends on the speed of the uniform technical progress, i.e. on the magnitude of the "investment effect" of new inventions. With the increase of the speed of the uniform technical progress both the positive and the negative effect rise in the same proportion and, consequently, so does $L(t)$, being the balance of these two effects.

From the latter it follows that the relation of the long-run net investment caused by $L(t)$ to the net investment in the preceding long period increases with the speed of technical progress. For $L(t)$ rises with the latter and net investment caused by $L(t)$ is the larger the greater is $L(t)$ (see p. 81). There will thus be a certain speed of technical progress which makes current long-run investment equal to the past long-run investment. The uniform technical progress then causes the capital accumulation of the past period to continue at the same rate. If the speed of technical progress is higher the current long-run investment will be higher than that in the past, and thus the technical progress causes here a secular growth of the rate of investment. Finally, if the speed of technical progress is lower than that necessary to maintain the rate of net investment, this will cause a long-run fall in the latter and the system will then approach asymptotically a stationary situation in which long-run net investment is zero.

4. So far we have discussed only technical progress uniform with regard to investment. According to our definition an accelerated technical progress takes place if the balance of the effect of new inventions and " liquidation " of past inventions on investment is positive for an economy of a given size. In such a case the trend component $L(t)$ is positive, and consequently so is the resulting net investment, even if in the preceding long-run period the system was stationary (i.e. the long-run net investment was equal to zero). While if the economy was previously expanding $L(t)$ consists of two components, one resulting from the acceleration of technical progress and the other from the preceding expansion of the system. If technical progress is retarded with regard to investment $L(t)$ is negative if the economy was stationary in the preceding long-run period; while if the economy was previously expanding $L(t)$ is the balance of the positive component resulting from this expansion and a negative one due to the slowing down of the technical progress.

Imagine now that in the initial long period technical progress is accelerated and this causes $L(t)$ and consequently net investment to be positive. Imagine further that after this period technical progress is uniform but the speed which it has reached is sufficient at least to maintain the rate of net investment of the preceding period. We shall then have a continuous trend created entirely by technical progress. *This pattern is likely to have played an important rôle in the development of capitalist economies.*

Imagine now on the other hand that after a period of expansion technical progress is slowing down (with regard to investment) over the period considered. This may occur, for instance, because of the formation of industrial monopolies which hamper the application of new inventions; or it may be the result of concentrating of technical progress on " scientific organization " of labour. This retardation of technical progress with regard to investment depresses $L(t)$ and thus the net investment in the period considered. In addition, the speed of technical progress is reduced; if it has fallen appreciably below the level which is necessary to maintain the rate of net investment in the future at the level of the period considered—net investment will rapidly approach zero in the subsequent period and the expansion of the system will come to a standstill.

5. There emerge out of our analysis, as the chief determinants of investment in the long run, changes in capitalists' consumption, rentiers' savings and innovations.

It should be noted that the limitations imposed on our analysis by simplifying assumptions prevented such factors as capital exports, budget deficits and gold production from being taken into consideration, although they definitely played a very important rôle in the development of single capitalist economies.

For Product Safety Concerns and Information please contact our EU
representative GPSR@taylorandfrancis.com Taylor & Francis Verlag GmbH,
Kaufingerstraße 24, 80331 München, Germany

Printed and bound by CPI Group (UK) Ltd, Croydon, CR0 4YY
08/05/2025
01864459-0001